Literary Analysis
for Enrichment

PLATINUM

Upper Saddle River, New Jersey
Glenview, Illinois
Needham, Massachusetts

Prentice
Hall

CONTENTS

UNIT 4: TURNING POINTS

UNIT 5: EXPANDING HORIZONS

UNIT 6: SHORT STORIES

UNIT 7: NONFICTION

UNIT 8: DRAMA

UNIT 9: POETRY

UNIT 10: EPICS AND LEGENDS

Name ____ Date ____________________

"Contents of a Dead Man's Pocket" by Jack Finney

Literary Analysis: Connecting Elements of a Short Story

1. The **plot** of a story is a series of related events moving from a problem to a solution. A plot often begins with **exposition,** which presents the characters and the situation, including the **conflict.** The conflict, the source of tension in a story, is a struggle between opposing people or forces. The conflict may be either **external,** between a character and another character or an outside force, or **internal,** within a character's mind. The conflict builds to a **climax,** the turning point of the story. Following the climax, the **resolution** shows how the problems are worked out. The plot may also have **complications,** events that stand in the way of resolving the conflict.

    a. Describe the major conflict in "Contents of a Dead Man's Pocket."

    ____

    ____

    b. Explain what complicates the opening situation.

    ____

    ____

    c. What is the moment of climax in the story?

    ____

    ____

    d. Why does the story continue after Tom gets safely back into the apartment?

    ____

    ____

2. **Characters** are the people, and in some cases animals, involved in the action of a story. A writer can reveal a character's personality through a variety of techniques, including direct statements about the character, the character's actions and comments, and what other characters say about the character. Briefly describe the main character of Finney's story, and discuss how his personality is revealed. Then explain how he changes as a result of the events in the story.

    ____

    ____

    ____

3. The **setting** is the time and place of the events in the story. Explain why the setting is a critical element of Finney's story.

    ____

    ____

4. **Theme** is the general idea about life that the author wants to communicate. Sometimes, the theme is revealed directly. More often, the theme is revealed indirectly through the characters and events in the story. State the theme of "Contents of the Dead Man's Pockets," and identify how it is revealed.

    ____

    ____

                    Literary Analysis for Enrichment   **1**

"View From the Summit" by Edmund Hillary
"The Dream Comes True" from *The Tiger of the Snows*
by Tenzing Norgay

Literary Analysis: Theme

The authors of "View From the Summit" and "The Dream Comes True" have different perspectives about their experiences on Mount Everest. These perspectives provide clues to the theme of each work. A **theme** is a literary work's central message or insight into life. It is a generalization about people or about life that the writer expresses. Sometimes, the theme is stated directly. Other times, you have to draw conclusions about the theme by reading between the lines.

DIRECTIONS: Use the passages in the following chart to help you state a major theme in "View From the Summit" and in "The Dream Comes True." Then answer the questions that follow.

Selection	Theme
"View From the Summit" 1. Almost under our feet it seemed, was the famous North Col and the East Rongbuk Glacier, where so many epic feats of courage and endurance were performed by the earlier British Everest expeditions . . . It was a sobering thought to remember how often these men had reached 28,000 feet without the benefits of our modern equipment and reasonably efficient oxygen sets.	
"The Dream Comes True" 2. I have asked myself, "What will future generations think of us if we allow the facts of our achievement to stay shrouded in mystery?" . . . And each time . . . the answer was the same: "Only the truth is good enough for the future."	

3. What do both authors' themes say about courage?

____

____

4. How do you think Norgay's theme might have been different if he had written his autobiography before Hillary's?

____

____

Name ____ Date _______________

"The Monkey's Paw" by W. W. Jacobs
"The Bridegroom" by Alexander Pushkin

Literary Analysis: Comparing a Short Story and a Narrative Poem

"The Monkey's Paw" and "The Bridegroom" are two different types of narratives—pieces of literature that tell a story. "The Monkey's Paw" is a **short story,** a brief fictional narrative. "The Bridegroom" is a **narrative poem,** a poem that tells a story. Like a short story, a narrative poem has one or more characters, a setting, a conflict, and a series of events that come to a conclusion. However, language and sound generally assume a more significant role in narrative poems than in short stories.

1. Briefly summarize the plots of both "The Monkey's Paw" and "The Bridegroom." Then note any similarities you find between the two plots.

2. How does Pushkin's use of verse in telling the story of "The Bridegroom" affect how you respond to the piece? Support your answers with passages from the poem.

3. Explain whether you think that the plot of "The Bridegroom" could serve as the basis of a gripping short story. Do you imagine that the piece would be more or less effective if it were rewritten as a short story? Explain.

4. Try rewriting an episode from "The Monkey's Paw" as a narrative poem. You may want to use "The Bridegroom" as a model for your poem.

Literary Analysis for Enrichment **3**

from "A Walk to the Jetty" from *Annie John* by Jamaica Kincaid

Literary Analysis: Setting

The **setting** is the time and place of the events in a story. In some stories, the setting is just the backdrop for the events. In "A Walk to the Jetty," however, the setting is a very important feature. Annie's environment triggers her flashbacks. The flashbacks, in turn, create different emotions in Annie. The setting also symbolizes Annie's change from childhood to adulthood.

DIRECTIONS: Read the descriptions of the settings in the following chart. Then identify Annie's emotions at that time and place. When you are done, answer the questions that follow.

Setting	How It Affects Annie's Emotions
1. passing by the seamstress's house	She is angry when she recalls how Miss Dulcie mistreated her.
2. passing by the library	
3. passing by the bank	
4. passing by the doctor's office	
5. on the launch	

6. Why do you think the half-hour walk must seem much longer to Annie?

____

____

____

7. How does the setting at the end of the story represent Annie's first steps toward independence?

____

____

____

Name ____ Date _______________

"The Masque of the Red Death" by Edgar Allan Poe

Literary Analysis: Figurative Language

Understanding **figurative language** can help you identify an writer's use of symbols. Types of figurative speech include similes, metaphors, and personification. Similes and metaphors set up comparisons between unlike objects and concepts; a simile uses the word *like* or *as* to make the comparison, while a metaphor makes the comparison directly. Personification occurs when a writer gives human traits to nonhuman things.

DIRECTIONS: For each passage in the following chart, identify the type of figurative language used. Then describe the idea, feeling, or state of mind that its use conveys to you. What associations and impressions are formed in your mind by the language? Then answer the question that follows.

Passage	Simile, Metaphor, or Personification	Idea, Feeling, or State of Mind Conveyed
1. The courtiers . . . bid defiance to contagion. The external world could take care of itself.	personification	shows how the wealthy have no feelings toward the poor and suffering
2. The pestilence raged most furiously abroad.		
3. brazen lungs of the clock		
4. But these other apartments were densely crowded, and in them beat feverishly the heart of life.		
5. [The Red Death] had come like a thief in the night.		
6. And the life of the ebony clock went out with that of the last of the gay.		

7. How does the author's use of figurative language help create a somber mood?

____

____

____

　　　　　　　　　　　　　　　Literary Analysis for Enrichment　**5**

"Spring and All" by William Carlos Williams
"Fear" by Gabriela Mistral
"The street" by Octavio Paz

Literary Analysis: Comparing Symbols

In poetry, a **symbol** is a person, place, object, or event that stands for something else. For example, the eagle is a symbol for the United States. Poets often use symbols to teach a lesson. You can examine the imagery, or descriptive language, to help you understand a poem's symbolism.

DIRECTIONS: Explain the symbols in the poems listed in the following chart. First, tell what the symbol represents. Then tell how it helps to teach a lesson. When you are done, answer the questions that follow.

Symbol	What Symbol Represents	How Symbol Helps Teach a Lesson
"Spring and All" 1. the stiff curl of wildcarrot leaf		
"Fear" 2. a swallow in flight		
"The street" 3. a dark and doorless street		

4. Compare the symbolism of the three poems. Which poem has the most uplifting symbolism? Explain.

____

____

____

5. How does imagery help you understand a poem's symbolism? Use two of the poems above as examples.

____

____

____

6. Choose one of the things listed in the chart. What else could it symbolize in a different context? Explain.

____

____

____

Name ____ Date _______________

"Two Friends" by Guy de Maupassant
"Damon and Pythias" retold by William F. Russell

Literary Analysis: Comparing Climax

Remember that a **climax,** or the high point, of a story can be expected or unexpected, depending on clues the writer provides. Identifying and comparing climaxes can help you better understand and enjoy what you read.

DIRECTIONS: In the following chart, briefly describe the climax of each story from this theme. Tell whether it is expected or unexpected, and why. Then answer the questions that follow.

Story	Climax	Expected or Unexpected? Why?
1. "Two Friends"	when the soldier threatens to kill the two men if they don't provide the password	expected, because the author gives hints that the enemy is ruthless
2. "Damon and Pythias"		
3. "Contents of the Dead Man's Pocket"		
4. "The Monkey's Paw"		
5. "The Masque of the Red Death"		

6. Which conflict was the most exciting? Why?

____

____

7. Suppose you were in one of the climactic situations. How would you respond to the tension?

____

____

from *In Commemoration: One Million Volumes* by Rudolfo A. Anaya

Literary Analysis: Denotation and Connotation

A writer chooses words carefully to communicate his or her purpose for writing. You can determine a writer's purpose by looking at story details and thinking about their denotations and connotations. A **denotation** is a word's literal meaning; a **connotation** is the set of ideas associated with a word. Words can have positive, negative, or neutral connotations, which are often specific to a culture or particular to the writer's own experience.

DIRECTIONS: Find important words in *In Commemoration* and list them in the chart. Use a dictionary to write each word's denotation. Then tell what its connotation is and why you think so. The first one has been done for you. Then answer the question that follows.

Word	Denotation (use dictionary)	Connotation (tell why)
1. imagination	the act of forming a mental picture of something that is not present	positive; it suggests the author is creative
2.		
3.		
4.		
5.		
6.		

7. Why do you think authors of personal essays use words with strong connotations?

____

____

____

____

"How Much Land Does a Man Need?" by Leo Tolstoy

Literary Analysis: Irony

A parable often contains irony, because the lesson of the story may be obvious to readers but not to the main character—at least until it's too late. **Irony** refers to literary techniques used by a writer to portray differences between appearance and reality, expectation and result, or meaning and intention. In **dramatic irony,** there is a contradiction between what a character thinks and what the reader knows to be true. In **irony of situation,** an event occurs that directly contradicts the expectations of the characters or the reader.

DIRECTIONS: Often, an event in a story is ironic only in hindsight. Complete the following chart by telling why each example listed from Tolstoy's story is ironic. The first one has been answered for you. When you are finished, answer the question that follows.

Story Event	Why It's Ironic
1. Pahom says, "If I had plenty of land, I shouldn't fear the Devil himself!"	The devil is listening and will tempt Pahom by giving him land.
2. Pahom is angry when he gets fined by the woman's manager, because he is careful with his animals.	
3. Pahom's heart fills with joy as he looks at his land.	
4. Pahom is ten times better off in the Volga than he had been.	
5. Pahom thinks he is tricking the Bashkir chief by getting a great deal on the land.	
6. Pahom dies of exhaustion after marking off a huge area of land.	

7. How does irony make the parable's moral more meaningful? Explain.

____

____

____

____

Unit 2: Striving for Success

"Success is counted sweetest" and **"I dwell in Possibility—"**
by Emily Dickinson
"Uncoiling" by Pat Mora
"Columbus Dying" by Vassar Miller

Literary Analysis: Tone

The **tone** of a poem is the poet's attitude toward his or her audience and subject. Tone usually can be described by a single adjective, such as *formal* or *informal, nostalgic, bitter,* or *ironic.* A poem's tone often can help you infer a poem's theme. To determine the tone of a poem, think about the poet's choice of words and images and what these details evoke.

DIRECTIONS: Describe the tone of each of the poems in the following chart. Then, support your responses using details from each of the poems. The first one has been done for you. When you are finished, answer the question that follows.

Poem	Tone	Detail(s) That Evoke the Tone
1. "Success is counted sweetest"	regretful	A dying soldier agonizes as he hears the sounds of triumph.
2. "I dwell in Possibility—"		
3. "Uncoiling"		
4. "Columbus Dying"		

5. Why do you think a poet might want to have a consistent tone throughout a short poem?

____

____

6. Choose the poem whose tone fits in best with the theme "Striving for Success." Explain your choice.

____

____

from *My Left Foot* by Christy Brown

Literary Analysis: Conflict

A **conflict** is a struggle between opposing forces. In an **external conflict,** a character struggles against an outside force. In an **internal conflict,** a character is in conflict with himself or herself. An autobiography can have more than one conflict, with some conflicts more important than others. The most significant conflicts often are resolved during critical moments in the plot.

DIRECTIONS: In the following chart, list an external conflict and an internal conflict in *My Left Foot.* Then identify how each conflict is resolved. When you are finished, answer the questions that follow.

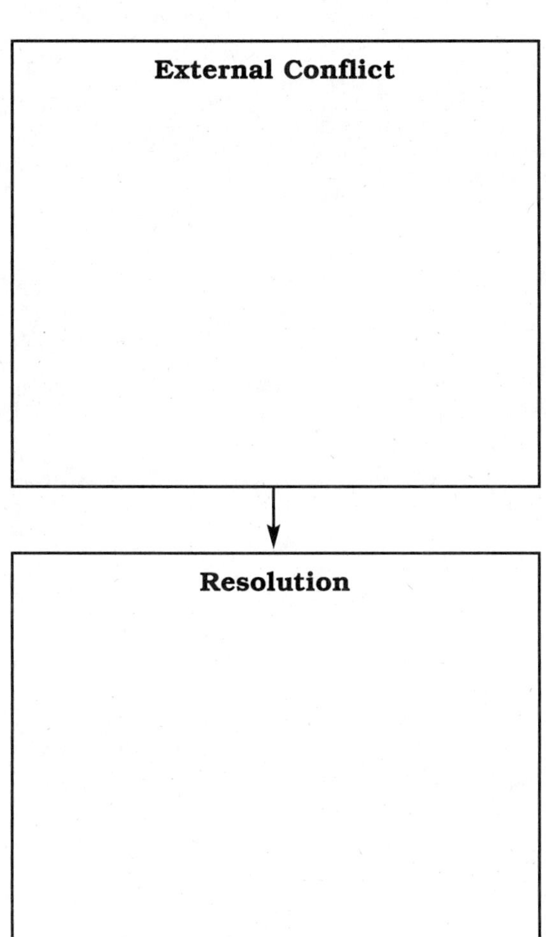

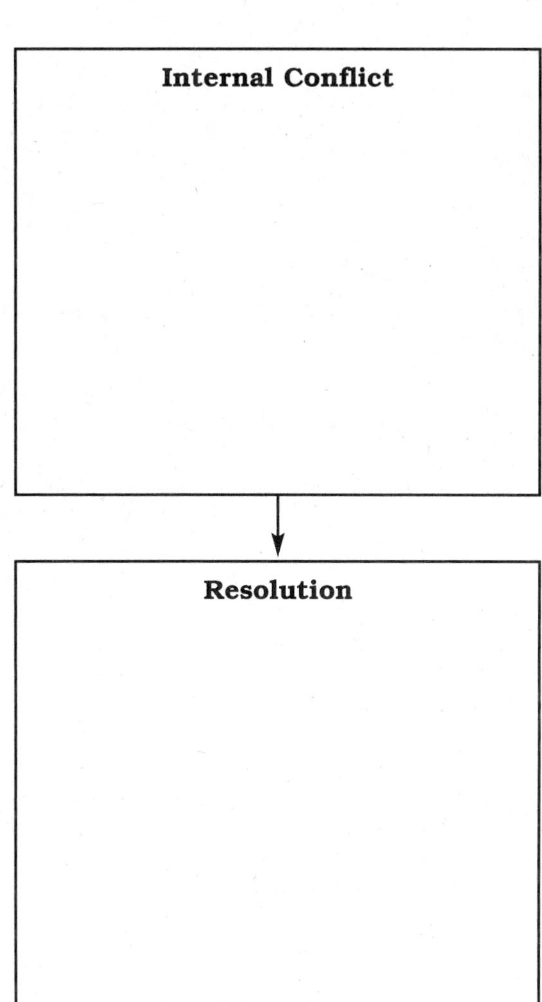

1. Which conflict is more important? Why do you think so?

____

____

2. Why is Christy's mother important to both conflicts?

____

____

   Literary Analysis for Enrichment   **11**

Literary Analysis: Comparing Anecdotes

An **anecdote** is a brief story about an interesting, amusing, or strange event. Writers usually use anecdotes to entertain or to make a point. You can learn a great deal about a character's personality by paying attention to the details in an anecdote. Note who is telling the anecdote, and why.

DIRECTIONS: In the following Venn diagram, compare and contrast the anecdote about GL and the horse in "A Visit to Grandmother" and the one about Christy and the chalk in *My Left Foot.* List at least three significant items for each portion of the digram. When you are finished, answer the questions that follow.

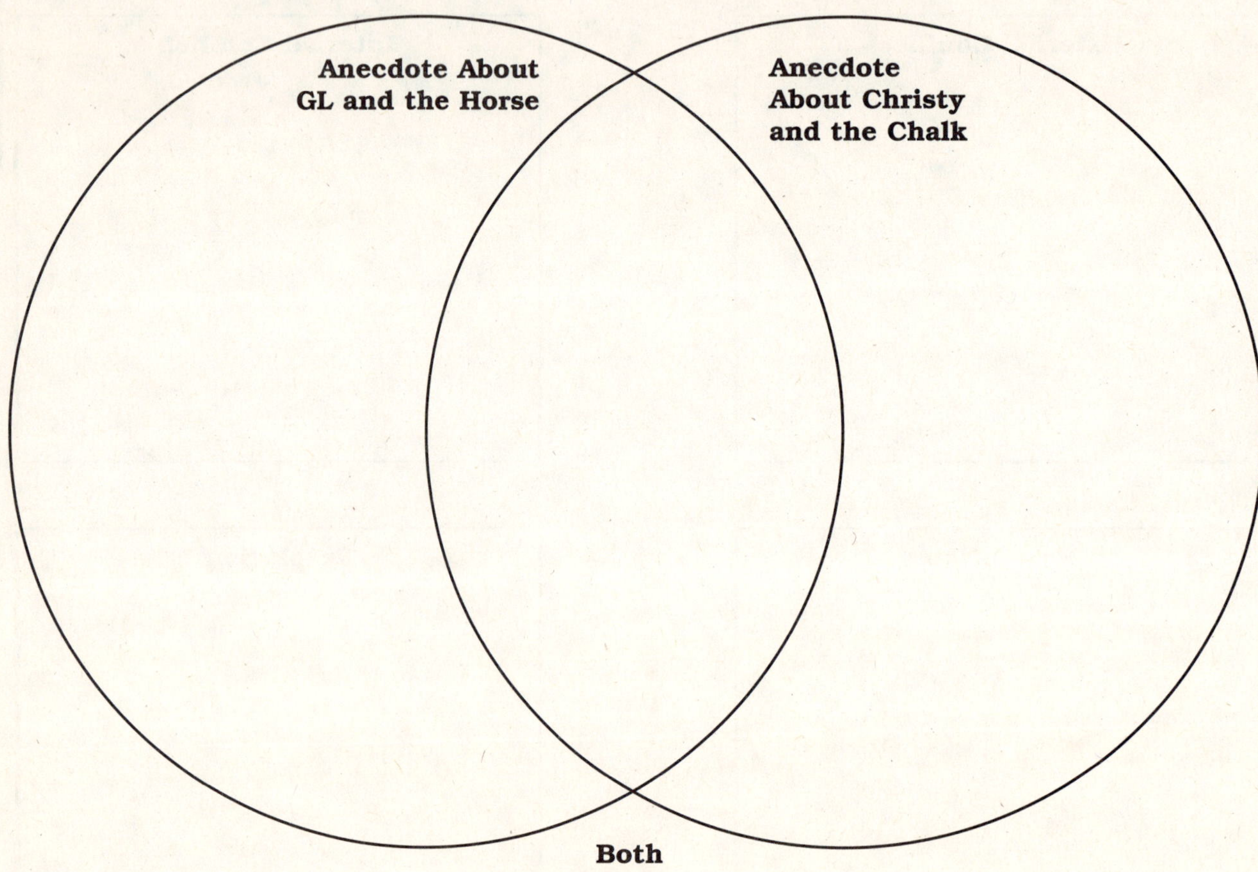

1. Why do you think an anecdote is a good way to share an author's message?

____

____

2. What is the tone of each anecdote? How can you tell?

____

____

"Mowing" and **"After Apple-Picking"** by Robert Frost
"Style" and **"At Harvesttime"** by Maya Angelou

Literary Analysis: Repetition

If you pay attention to repetition in a poem, you often can find clues to its tone. **Repetition** includes repeated words, alliteration, assonance, rhyme, and rhythm. A poet often uses repetition for its musical effect and to emphasize important ideas and details.

DIRECTIONS: Classify the kind of repetition found in the examples listed in the following chart. Then describe what you think the purpose of the repetition is. The first one has been done for you. When you have completed the chart, answer the question that follows.

Poem	Example(s) of Repetition	Type(s) of Repetition	Purpose(s)
1. "Success is counted sweetest"	On whose forbidden ear The distant strains of triumph Burst agonized and clear!	rhyme	It draws your attention to the sadness of hearing the enemy's triumphant sounds.
2. "I dwell in Possibility—"	Of Chambers as the Cedars—		
3. "Uncoiling"	she scratches . . . She sighs . . . She spews . . .		
4. "Columbus Dying"	No dragons gnawing on drowned soldiers' brains.		
5. "Mowing"	What was it it whispered? . . . And that was why it whispered . . .		
6. "After Apple-Picking"	Of load on load of apples coming in.		

7. Why can you appreciate repetition in poems more easily if you read them aloud?

____

____

____

"The Apple Tree" by Katherine Mansfield

Literary Analysis: Dialect

Writers sometimes make allusions to other literary works or reference other sources in their own work. Writers also try to center their stories in specific places and times. Readers then can enjoy the stories on more than one level. One way a writer can center the story is by using **dialect,** or the form of language spoken by a particular group of people or by people in a particular region.

DIRECTIONS: Complete each row of the following chart by identifying the setting of each story and the meaning of each example of dialect. The names in parentheses show the speaker. The first one has been done for you. When you are finished, answer the question that follows.

Title	Example of Dialect	Setting	Meaning of Dialect
1. "The Apple Tree"	"Great Scott!" said the friend again.	New Zealand	The friend is excited about the apple tree.
2. "The Apple Tree"	"They're wonderful apples! Tiptop!" (Father)		
3. "The Apple Tree"	"Don't *bolt* it!" said he. (Father)		
4. "A Visit to Grandmother"	"What they tell you about me, Chig? They tell you I'm all laid up?" (Grandmother)		
5. "A Visit to Grandmother"	"Oh, you talking about that crazy horse GL brung home that time." (Grandmother)		
6. "A Visit to Grandmother"	"Sure, come on, Mama," GL says. "There ain't nothing to be fidgety about."		

7. How does the use of dialect help you understand a story's characters and setting?

____

____

____

____

"Africa" by David Diop
"Old Song" Traditional
"All" by Bei Dao
"Also All" by Shu Ting
from *The Analects* by Confucius

Literary Analysis: Comparing Persuasive Essays

The excerpt from *The Analects* is a type of nonfiction **persuasive essay,** since Confucius wants you to agree with his viewpoint. One way he does this is to include aphorisms. Writers can also try to persuade by using metaphors, personal experiences, or supporting details.

DIRECTIONS: Compare *The Analects* with other the persuasive essays in this section. For each example in the following chart, list the author's viewpoint, supporting examples or reasons, and whether you think the essay is effective. When you have completed the chart, answer the questions that follow.

Essay	Author's Viewpoint	Reasons or Examples	Is the Essay Effective?
1. *In Commemoration*			
2. "Style"			
3. "At Harvesttime"			
4. *The Analects*			

5. Why might a writer want to persuade readers through a nonfiction essay rather than through fiction?

____

____

6. Which essay did you enjoy the most? Why?

____

____

"Through the Tunnel" by Doris Lessing

Literary Analysis: Resolving Internal and External Conflicts

Conflict is a struggle or battle between opposing forces in a story. In an **internal conflict,** a character struggles within himself or herself over opposing beliefs, needs, or feelings. In an **external conflict,** the character struggles against an outside opponent, such as another person, force, or organization. In both cases, the character must make choices and take actions to resolve the conflict, which is referred to as the **resolution** of the story.

DIRECTIONS: In the following web, write a resolution for each conflict in "Through the Tunnel." Identify another conflict and add it to the empty spoke.

1. **Internal Conflict:** Jerry was torn between staying with his mother and exploring a wild, rocky bay.

   Resolution:

2. **Internal Conflict:** Jerry spotted his mom on the beach but suddenly felt lonely.

   Resolution:

3. **Internal Conflict:** Jerry wanted to be with the group of boys but couldn't figure out how to fit in.

   Resolution:

Jerry's Conflicts

4. **Internal Conflict:** Jerry fears the diving rock but also feels compelled to conquer it.

   Resolution:

5. **External Conflict:** Jerry fights against the diving rock.

   Resolution:

6.

"The Dog That Bit People" by James Thurber

Literary Analysis: Comparing Narratives

A **narrative** is writing that tells a story in fiction, nonfiction, poetry, or drama. James Thurber's "The Dog That Bit People" is narrative nonfiction—with a twist. Thurber skillfully uses humor to string a series of amusing anecdotes into an essay.

DIRECTIONS: The following chart lists three types of narratives. Find an example in Unit 1 or 2 of each type. Write the name of the work and a short justification for each of your choices.

Type of Narrative	Selection	Reason
1. fiction		
2. nonfiction	"The Dog That Bit People"	It tells a story and is based on actual events.
3. poetic		

"Conscientious Objector" by Edna St. Vincent Millay
"A Man" by Nina Cassian
"The Weary Blues" by Langston Hughes
"Jazz Fantasia" by Carl Sandburg

Literary Analysis: Comparing the Use of Symbols

The tone of a poem conveys the poet's attitude toward the poem's subject. The poet communicates tone through words, images, and the use of symbols. A **symbol** is anything that stands for something else. A symbol can represent a concrete object or an abstract idea. A flag, for instance, symbolizes a country. Diamonds or gold often symbolize wealth. Writers often come up with their own symbols. Looking for the symbols in a piece of writing can help you understand its meaning more fully.

DIRECTIONS: Complete the following chart to compare how symbols are used by different writers. For each story or poem in the chart, interpret the symbol that is listed. Then identify and interpret another symbol from the story or poem. For the fourth item, choose a story or poem you already have read from your textbook.

Selection	Symbol	What the Symbol Stands For
1. "Conscientious Objector"	a. black boy b. Death	all people who are oppressed "Death" stands for war.
2. "A Man"	a. half a harvest b.	
3. "Through the Tunnel"	a. the diving rock b.	
4.	a. b.	

"Like the Sun" by R. K. Narayan
"Tell all the Truth but tell it slant—" by Emily Dickinson

Literary Analysis: Verbal Irony

In the story "Like the Sun," R. K. Narayan uses irony, a literary technique that portrays differences between appearances and reality, expectation and result, or meaning and intention. Emily Dickinson's poem "Tell all the Truth but tell it slant—" is built on an ironic theme: Tell the truth, but with a spin so people can handle it. Throughout the poem, Dickinson uses **verbal irony,** or words that suggest the opposite of what is meant, to create "clashes" that make her point.

DIRECTIONS: For each pair of passages listed in the following chart, explain the ironic "clash." The first one has been done for you.

	Irony	
1. "Tell all the Truth . . ."	Dickinson says to tell the truth, but in a way that isn't too truthful.	". . . but tell it slant—"
2. "Success . . ."		". . . in Circuit lies"
3. "As Lightning . . ."		". . . to the Children eased With explanation kind"
4. "The truth must dazzle gradually . . ."		". . . Or every man be blind—"

Literary Analysis for Enrichment **19**

Unit 3: Clashing Forces

"Hearts and Hands" by O. Henry
"The Fish" by Elizabeth Bishop

Literary Analysis: Characterization

Characterization is the way writers develop their characters. In most stories, writers develop their characters in straightforward ways. Sometimes writers simply tell the reader about the characters. Or writers let readers figure out the characters for themselves, based on their looks, actions, and interactions with other characters.

However, in a story or a poem that has a surprise ending, a writer must work a little magic with characterization. The writer must deliberately mislead the readers so they believe things about the characters that aren't true. Then the truth can be a surprise in the end.

DIRECTIONS: In the first chart, identify the misleading details each writers uses when characterizing the different characters in "Hearts and Hands" and "The Fish." In the second chart, identify clues each writer provides to set up the surprise ending.

Misleading Details in "Hearts and Hands"	Misleading Details in "The Fish"
1. Mr. Easton easily fit the mold of a "professional" type of person, as a marshal might be.	6. The speaker was holding the fish half out of the water, as if in the process of pulling it into the boat.
2.	7.
3.	8.
4.	9.
5.	10.

Clues to the Surprise Ending in "Hearts and Hands"	Clues to the Surprise Ending in "The Fish"
11. Mr. Easton was embarrassed when Miss Fairchild recognized him.	14. The speaker describes the fish in a way that's respectful.
12.	15.
13.	16.

from *Desert Exile: The Uprooting of a Japanese-American Family*
by Yoshiko Uchida
Speech on the Japanese American Internment by Gerald Ford

Literary Analysis: Writer's Purpose and Autobiography

One of Uchida's purposes in writing her book *Desert Exile* is to tell her personal story. Her book is an **autobiography**—a work of nonfiction in which a person tells the story of his or her own life. An autobiography can tell about a person's entire life or only a part of it, as Uchida does here. Because an autobiography is told from the perspective of the person who experience it, you are able to look through the writer's own eyes at the events and situations.

DIRECTIONS: Next to each statement listed in the chart below, identify Uchida's purpose for including it in her autobiography. The first one has been done for you.

Statement	Author's Purpose for Including It
1. It had rained the day before and the hundreds of people who had trampled on the track had turned it into a miserable mass of slippery mud.	Maybe the author wanted to us to imagine the complications of hundreds of people living together in "camp-type" conditions. Maybe her words *miserable mass* describe the people, not just the mud.
2. That the stalls should have been called "apartments" was a euphemism so ludicrous it was comical.	
3. We spent much of the evening talking about food and the lack of it, a concern that grew obsessive over the next few weeks, when we were constantly hungry.	
4. I wrote to my non-Japanese friends in Berkeley shamelessly asking them to send us food, and they obliged with large cartons of cookies, nuts, dried fruit, and jams.	
5. Papa was coming home . . . but even as we hugged each other in joy, we didn't quite dare believe it until we actually saw him . . .	

Unit 3: Clashing Forces

"The Cabuliwallah" by Rabindranath Tagore

Literary Analysis: Comparing Relationships Between Characters

When you read, it is helpful to examine the **relationships between characters.** Relationships are dynamic—they change according to feelings, events, or the passage of time. When you pay attention to changing relationships, you can more clearly see the themes and messages that the writer is developing.

DIRECTIONS: Answer the questions in the right column of the following chart. Use the passages and statement in the left column to help you.

"Through the Tunnel"	
1. "Why, [Jerry], would you rather not come with me?" . . . Contrition sent him running after her. And yet, as he ran, he looked back over his shoulder at the wild bay.	Why do you think Jerry doesn't want to hurt his mother's feelings? By the end of the story, does Jerry still feel protective of his mother? How can you tell?
"Like the Sun"	
2. Sekhar received a note from the headmaster: "Please see me before you go home." Sekhar said to himself: It must be about these horrible test papers . . . He had shirked this work for weeks, feeling all the time as if a sword were hanging over his head.	Based on what you know at this point in the story, how does Sekhar feel about his relationship with the headmaster? Answer the question above at the end of the story.
"Hearts and Hands"	
3. Miss Fairchild is interested in renewing and pursuing a relationship with Mr. Easton.	Which passage(s) from the story support this description of the relationship?

from *Speak, Memory* by Vladimir Nabokov

Literary Analysis: Comparing Personal Narratives

In a **personal narrative,** an writer tells you about his or her life from the first-person point of view. In Unit 3, you read Yoshiko Uchida's personal narrative about her experiences in a Japanese American internment camp. In this unit, you're reading about Vladimir Nabokov's early love of books and language. Both of these writers have purposes for writing, themes they develop, and ways they communicate their stories to you.

DIRECTIONS: Complete the following chart to analyze and compare these two personal narratives.

	Yoshiko Uchida	Vladimir Nabokov
1. What is the author's main purpose?		
2. What is the theme of this selection?		
3. Which selection is easier or more inviting to read than the other? Why?		
4. Does the writer do a good job of "painting" word pictures you can see as you read the story? Explain.		
5. On a scale of 1–10 (with 10 being the best), how would you rank each writer in terms of skill? Why?		
6. Which selection did you like better? Why?		

Unit 4: Turning Points

Name ____ Date _______________

"Games at Twilight" by Anita Desai

Literary Analysis: Developing Character as Symbols

In "Games at Twilight," Anita Desai develops characters as symbols. Each character represents a bigger concept or idea.

DIRECTIONS: In the first column of the following chart, explain what you think Ravi stands for in the story and then give five reasons to support your opinion. In the second column, develop a character who could be a symbol for a concept (such as freedom, oppression, youth, justice, wisdom, sadness, joy) that's important to you.

Ravi	Your character's name:
Is a symbol for:	Is a symbol for:
Support: 1.	What does your character look or act like? (Include age, gender, physical characteristics, typical behaviors and habits, type of clothing, attitude and so on.)
2.	
3.	How would you develop your character so people would know what he or she stands for? (Include ways of speaking, character traits, and consistent behaviors.)
4.	
5.	

Name ____ Date ________________

"The Bridge" by Leopold Staff
"The Old Stoic" by Emily Brontë
"I Am Not One of Those Who Left the Land" by Anna Akhmatova
"Speech During the Invasion of Constantinople" by Empress Theodora

Literary Analysis: Comparing Authors' Purposes

Authors write for a variety of reasons. Sometimes, an author wants to persuade you to agree with his or her beliefs, or to inform you about important information. Other times, an author wants to express an opinion or to entertain you. Whatever the author's purpose, it affects the content and style of his or her writing. By paying careful attention to the kinds of details an author uses, as well as the attitude he or she takes toward his or her subject, you can determine the author's purpose.

DIRECTIONS: Choose two works from this section and complete the following chart to compare the authors' purposes.

	Title:	Title:
1. What is the subject of the work?		
2. Whom is the author addressing?		
3. What details does the author include?		
4. What is the author's attitude toward his or her subject?		
5. What is the author's purpose? (Remember that an author may write a work for more than one reason.)		

Literary Analysis for Enrichment **25**

"The Good Deed" by Pearl S. Buck

Literary Analysis: Setting and Character

The **setting** of a literary work refers to the time and place of the action in the story. Time can include a specific time of day, season, or year, in addition to the historical period. Place can involve the social, economic, or cultural environment beyond the actual geographical region. In "The Good Deed," the dynamic character of Mrs. Pan is in conflict with her new surroundings, because America is so unlike her native China. Although the story is set in America, China plays a very important role in the story.

DIRECTIONS: In the first column of the following chart, describe Mrs. Pan's new home in America based on details in the story. Then, in the second column, describe the home she left behind in China. When you have finished, answer the question that follows.

America	China
The water tastes of metal and not of earth, and so the flavor of food is not the same.	

Mrs. Pan, a dynamic character, changes during the story. If the story continued, do you think her view of the setting would change too? Explain.

____

____

____

Name ____ Date _______________

"Thoughts of Hanoi" by Nguyen Thi Vinh
"Pride" by Dahlia Ravikovitch
"Auto Wreck" by Karl Shapiro
"Before the Law" by Franz Kafka

Literary Analysis: Comparing Theme

Poets often have used their craft to provide social commentary. Both Anna Akhmatova's "I Am Not One of Those Who Left the Land" and Nguyen Thi Vinh's "Thoughts of Hanoi" deal with the effects of war on the lives of people.

DIRECTIONS: Complete the following chart to compare the themes of Akhmatova's and Vinh's poems.

	"I Am Not One of Those Who Left the Land"	**"Thoughts of Hanoi"**
1. Where was the speaker during the war?		
2. Whom is the speaker addressing?		
3. What emotion is the speaker expressing?		
4. What is the theme of the poem?		

5. How are the two poems' themes similar? How are they different?

____

____

____

____

Unit 4: Turning Points

   Literary Analysis for Enrichment   **27**

"The Widow and the Parrot" by Virginia Woolf

Literary Analysis: Character

A **character** is a person or an animal who takes part in the action of a literary work. Clear and logical motives make a character more believable and engaging. There are two major types of characters: round characters show many different personality traits, both good and bad; flat characters only one side of themselves, either good or bad.

DIRECTIONS: Complete the following chart by identifying Mrs. Gage's good and/or bad traits. Then answer the question that follows.

Good Traits	Bad Traits
sent her brother a Christmas card every year, even though he didn't respond	doesn't seem sad that her brother is dead

Is Mrs. Gage a round character or a flat character? Explain.

____

____

____

"Civil Peace" by Chinua Achebe

Literary Analysis: Key Statements and Theme

Often, key statements can help to reveal the theme of a story. The **theme** is the central message about life that is communicated to the reader by the writer. The theme usually is an insight into life rather than a simple summary of the plot.

The theme of a story may be stated directly or implied by the author. When the theme is implied, you should ask yourself questions like these:

- What is the author trying to say?

- What lesson can I learn from the story?

- What message do I get from the way the characters deal with the situation?

DIRECTIONS: In the outside circles in the web below, write key statements from "Civil Peace." Then read those statements and think about what the theme of the story is. Write the theme in the center circle.

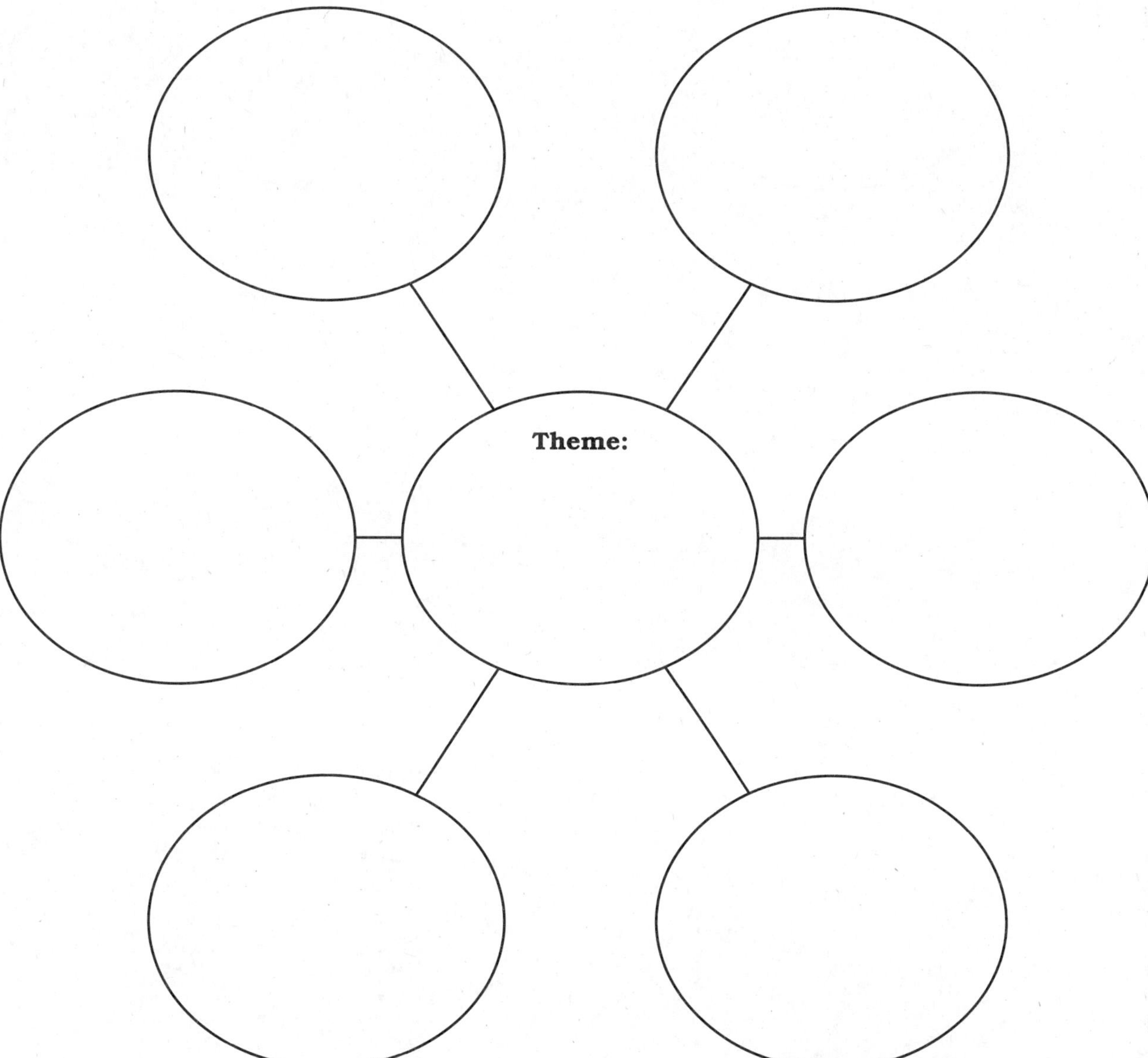

Unit 5: Expanding Horizons

"The Bean Eaters" by Gwendolyn Brooks
"How to React to Familiar Faces" by Umberto Eco

Literary Analysis: Mood

The tone of a work is directly related to its **mood,** or the feeling created in the reader. Often, the mood is suggested by a writer's descriptive details and can be described in one word, such as *somber, lighthearted,* or *fearful.* Most of the time, the writer's tone clearly sets the mood of the piece.

DIRECTIONS: As you read "The Bean Eaters," identify the mood of the poem and write it in the center circle of the following web. Then reread the poem and identify the descriptive details that suggest the mood of the work. Record these details in the outer circles. Be sure to support your answers.

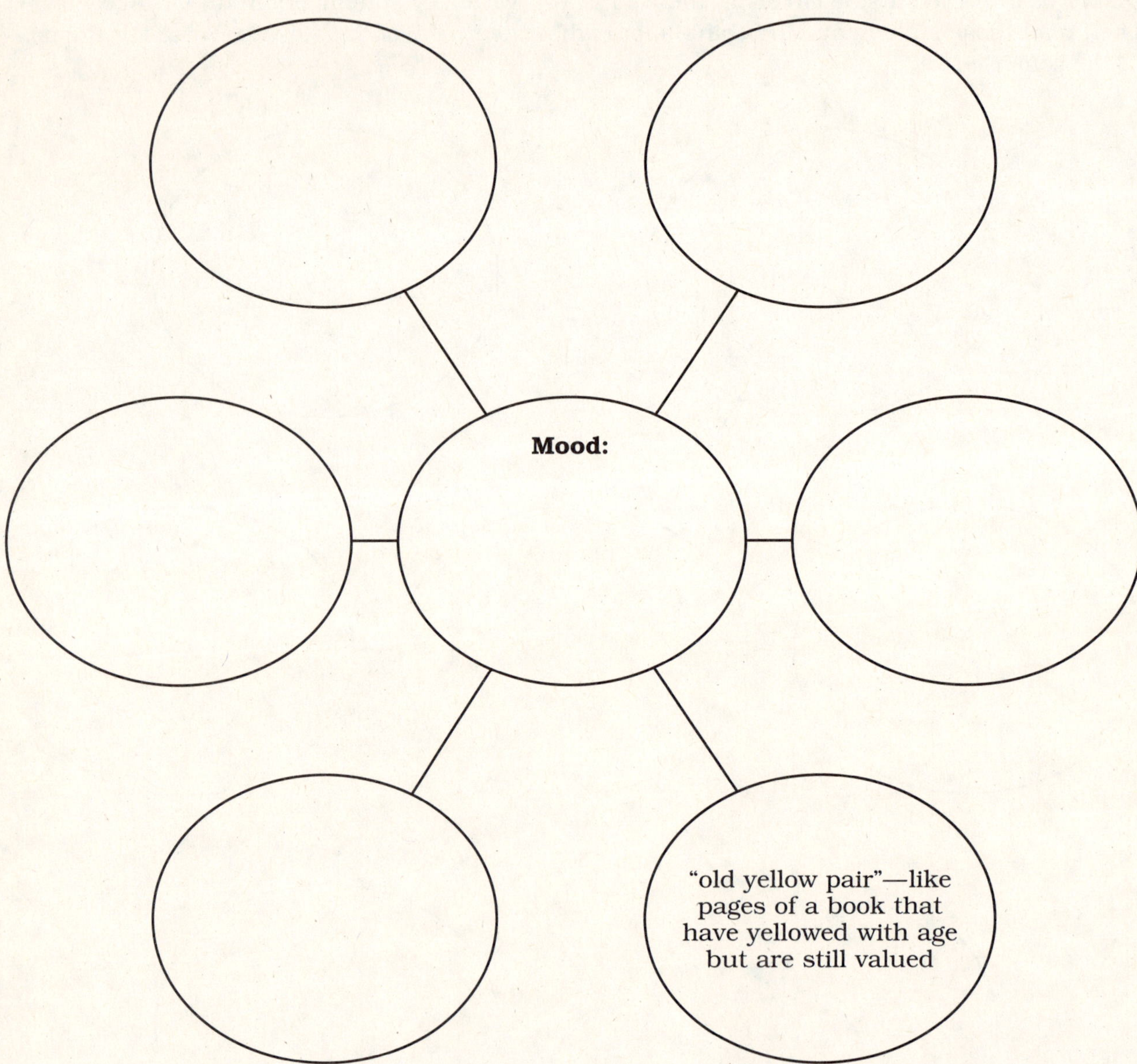

"A Picture From the Past: Emily Dickinson" by Reynolds Price
"What Makes a Degas a Degas?" by Richard Mühlberger

Literary Analysis: Comparing Descriptions

A **description** is a word picture of a person, place, or thing that writers use to create a particular image in the reader's mind. A writer usually uses descriptive details that appeal to some or all of your senses—sight, taste, touch, sound, and smell. Since Reynolds Price and Paul Mühlberger are both describing pictures, the details they use deal primarily with the sense of sight.

DIRECTIONS: Complete the following chart by identifying details from both essays that appeal to the senses.

Sense	"A Picture From the Past: Emily Dickinson"	"What Makes a Degas a Degas?"
Sight	homely girl	theater's public boxes and stalls
Other Senses	touch: picture is light in your hand	

"The Orphan Boy and the Elk Dog," a Blackfeet Myth

Literary Analysis: Myth and Setting

Setting is the time and place of a story. Since myths involve elements of the supernatural, the setting is an essential piece of the story. The time of "The Orphan Boy and the Elk Dog," as the beginning of the story tells you, is hundreds of years ago, before the Blackfeet had horses. The place is the plains of North America. However, the setting changes to accommodate the introduction of immortal beings into the story. They do not live among the humans, but rather in places where humans cannot live, thus making setting an important aspect of the story.

DIRECTIONS: Use the Venn diagram below to compare and contrast the real-world setting to the supernatural-world setting in "The Orphan Boy and the Elk Dog." In the overlapping section of both circles, write the similarities between the two worlds. Record the differences in the outer portion of each circle.

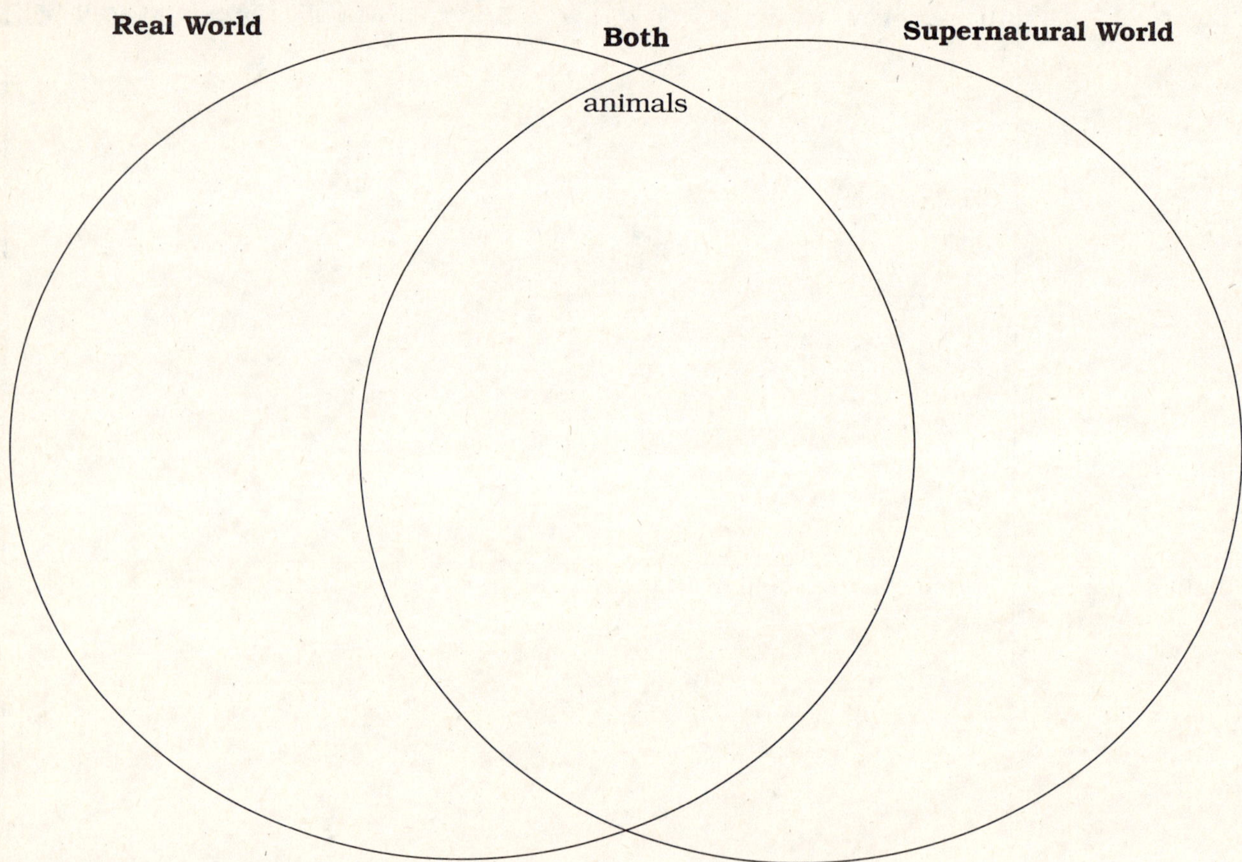

"The Street of the Cañon" from *Mexican Village* by Josephina Niggli

Literary Analysis: Comparing Narrators

The point of view of a story is determined by the **narrator,** the speaker or the character who is telling the story. The narrator can be a character in the story, known as a **first-person narrator.** The narrator can also be an outside observer who does not exist within the world of the story, and can reveal to the reader what all the characters think and feel. This is known as **third-person narration.**

DIRECTIONS: Identify the type of narrator used in each work listed in the following chart. Then decide whether a different type of narrator might have been more effective in telling the story. Be sure to explain your reasoning.

Selection	Type of Narrator	Better Narrator? Why?
1. "The Widow and the Parrot"	omniscient third person	This was the best choice because the narrator tells all characters' thoughts.
2. "Civil Peace"		
3. "How to React to Familiar Faces"		
4. "The Street of the Cañon"		

     Literary Analysis for Enrichment   **33**

"A Storm in the Mountains" by Alexander Solzhenitsyn
"In the Orchard" by Henrik Ibsen
"A Tree Telling of Orpheus" by Denise Levertov

Literary Analysis: Diction

The **diction** of a work refers to the writer's choice of words. When thinking about a writer's diction, pay attention to the vocabulary used and whether you think it is appropriate for the situation, as well as how vivid the language is. Both the denotations and connotations of words are important to consider when you are studying diction.

DIRECTIONS: Examine the diction in the following passages by answering the questions.

1. The voice of the thunder filled the gorge, drowning the ceaseless roar of the rivers.

   —"A Storm in the Mountains"

   Why do you think the author chose these words instead of just saying "the thunder was louder than the rivers"? What is the difference between the two? Which is more powerful? More meaningful? Why do you think so?

   ____

   ____

   ____

   ____

   ____

   ____

2. Will you ask about the fruitage
   In the season of the flowers?

   —"In the Orchard"

   What more is said with these words than if Ibsen had written, "Will you ask about the fruit crop in the spring?" Why would the author phrase the question with those words? What images do you get from them that you don't get from the rewritten question above?

   ____

   ____

   ____

   ____

   ____

   ____

Name _________________________________ Date _______________

"The Open Window" by Saki

Literary Analysis: Surprise Ending

All stories have similar plot structures. However, not all stories end the way you assume they're going to end. Sometimes, a story ends with am unexpected twist—a **surprise ending.** Most writers will hint at the surprise ending by providing clues along the way.

DIRECTIONS: Read each story event in the following chart. Then complete the chart by identifying clues from each event that suggest the surprise ending.

Story Event	Clues to Surprise Ending
1. Framton and the niece chat before Mrs. Sappleton comes in.	The niece asks strange questions, almost as if she is interrogating him.
2. The niece starts her story with, "You may wonder why we keep that window wide open on an October afternoon."	
3. The niece tells about the men disappearing on the hunt, and Framton appears to believe her.	
4. The aunt is brisk and cheerful, talking about hunting.	
5. Framton sees a look of horror on the niece's face as she stares in the direction of the returning men.	
6. Mrs. Sappleton explains who Framton is to the men.	
7. The niece tells a story about Framton being afraid of dogs.	

"Leiningen Versus the Ants" by Carl Stephenson

Literary Analysis: Rising Action and Climax

The conflict in a story sets in motion the **rising action** of the plot, which then leads to the **climax** of the story. The climax is the highest point of interest or suspense, and all the events leading up to the climax make up the rising action. In a short story, a majority of the action will consist of the rising action.

DIRECTIONS: Use the following diagram to identify plot events in the story that lead to the climax. Then identify the climax in item 11 and the ending of the story in item 12. Use the lines provided to record your answers.

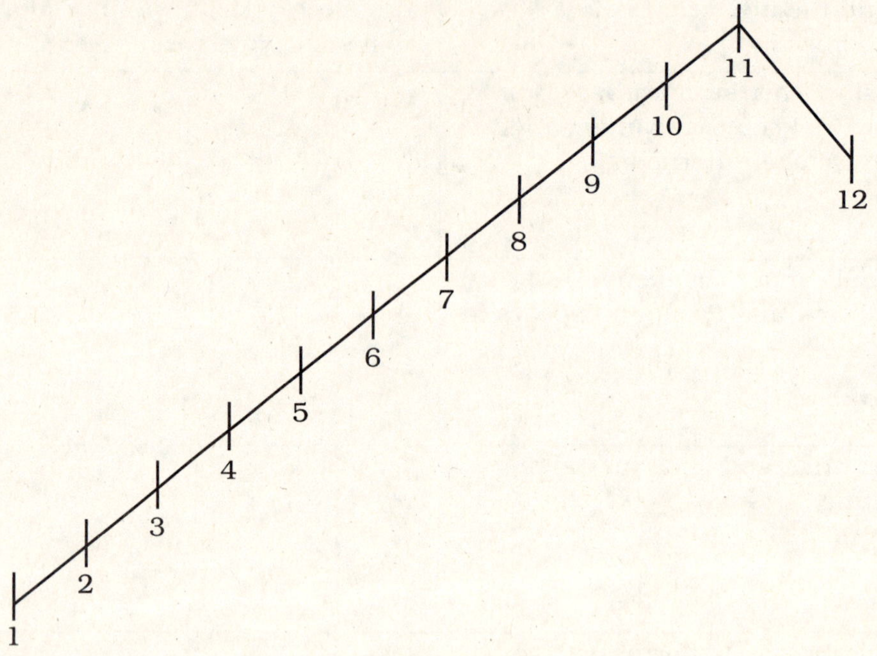

1. The ants surround the plantation and start trying to cross a water-filled ditch.

2. ___________________________________

3. ___________________________________

4. ___________________________________

5. ___________________________________

6. ___________________________________

7. ___________________________________

8. ___________________________________

9. ___________________________________

10. ___________________________________

11. ___________________________________

12. ___________________________________

Name ____ Date _______________

"By the Waters of Babylon" by Stephen Vincent Benét

Literary Analysis: Comparing Dialogue

Conversations between characters are referred to as **dialogue.** In general, an author uses dialogue to show more about a character and to advance the action of the story. Quotation marks are used to identify a speaker's exact words, and a new paragraph indicates a change of speaker.

DIRECTIONS: Answer the following questions.

1. How does the use of dialogue in "By the Waters of Babylon" reveal character?

____

____

____

____

____

2. How does the use of dialogue in "The Open Window" reveal character?

____

____

____

____

____

3. How does the dialogue in "Leiningen Versus the Ants" advance the action of the story? Give a specific example.

____

____

____

____

4. Is there one of these three pieces in which you would have liked to see more dialogue? Why?

____

____

____

____

____

"A Problem" by Anton Chekhov
"Luck" by Mark Twain

Literary Analysis: Comparing Monologues

Characters speak to each other in two primary ways—through dialogue and monologue. Dialogue is conversation between characters. A **monologue** is a speech delivered by one character.

DIRECTIONS: Answer the following questions.

1. Why do you think Chekhov described most of Ivan Markovitch's monologue rather than letting him speak it all? Would having Markovitch speak it all be more effective than the way Chekhov wrote it? Why or why not?

____

____

____

____

____

____

2. Twain uses two monologues in "Luck" to tell the story of Scoresby, a lucky fool. How effective is this technique? Would you get more out of the story if it was told in dialogue and description? Why or why not?

____

____

____

____

____

3. What other works in this unit use monologue to help tell the story?

____

____

____

____

____

____

Name ____ Date ___________________

"There Will Come Soft Rains" by Ray Bradbury
"The Garden of Stubborn Cats" by Italo Calvino

Literary Analysis: Short Story

A **short story** is a brief work of fiction. Writers of short stories must make every word they write work hard to communicate meaning; they must say more with fewer words. Because it is significantly shorter than a novel, a short story usually has one main character who faces a conflict that is resolved by the end of the story. In addition, a short story has only a limited amount of time and space in which to describe the setting. Usually, a short story is limited to one or two settings due to the limits of the genre's length.

DIRECTIONS: Choose either "There Will Come Soft Rains" or "The Garden of Stubborn Cats." Complete the following word web by identifying the characteristics of a short story using examples from the story you have selected.

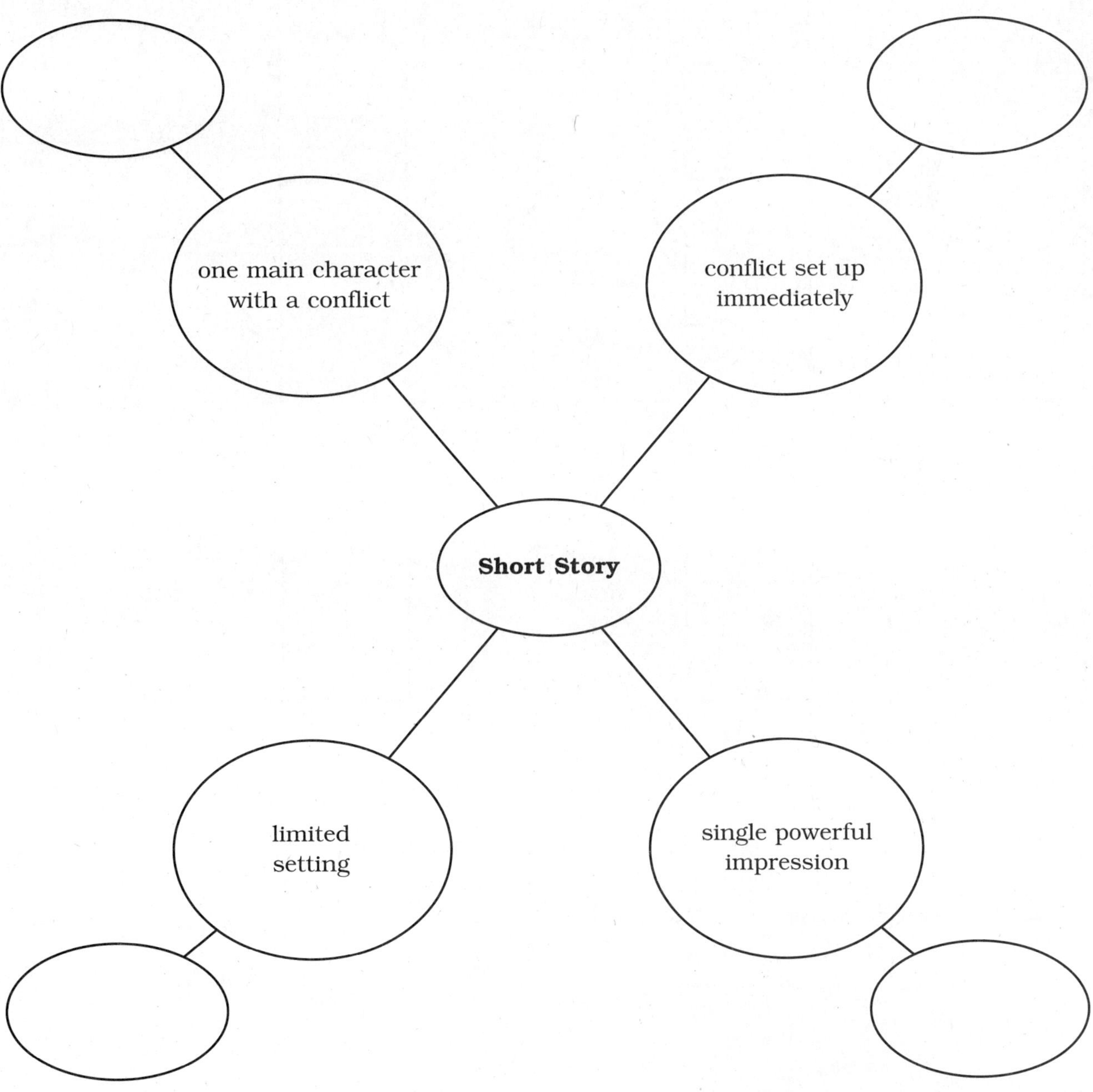

Literary Analysis for Enrichment   **39**

"The Princess and All the Kingdom" by Pär Lagerkvist
"The Censors" by Luisa Valenzuela

Literary Analysis: Characters

Both "The Princess and All the Kingdom" and "The Censors" deal with universal themes as shown through the actions and words of the **main characters.** Both main characters in these stories are **round;** that is, both their virtues and their faults are shown. In addition, these characters are **dynamic,** meaning that they have undergone some sort of change by the end of the story.

DIRECTIONS: In the following diagram, list each main character's traits at the beginning of the story, what event(s) cause him to change, and his traits after the life-changing event.

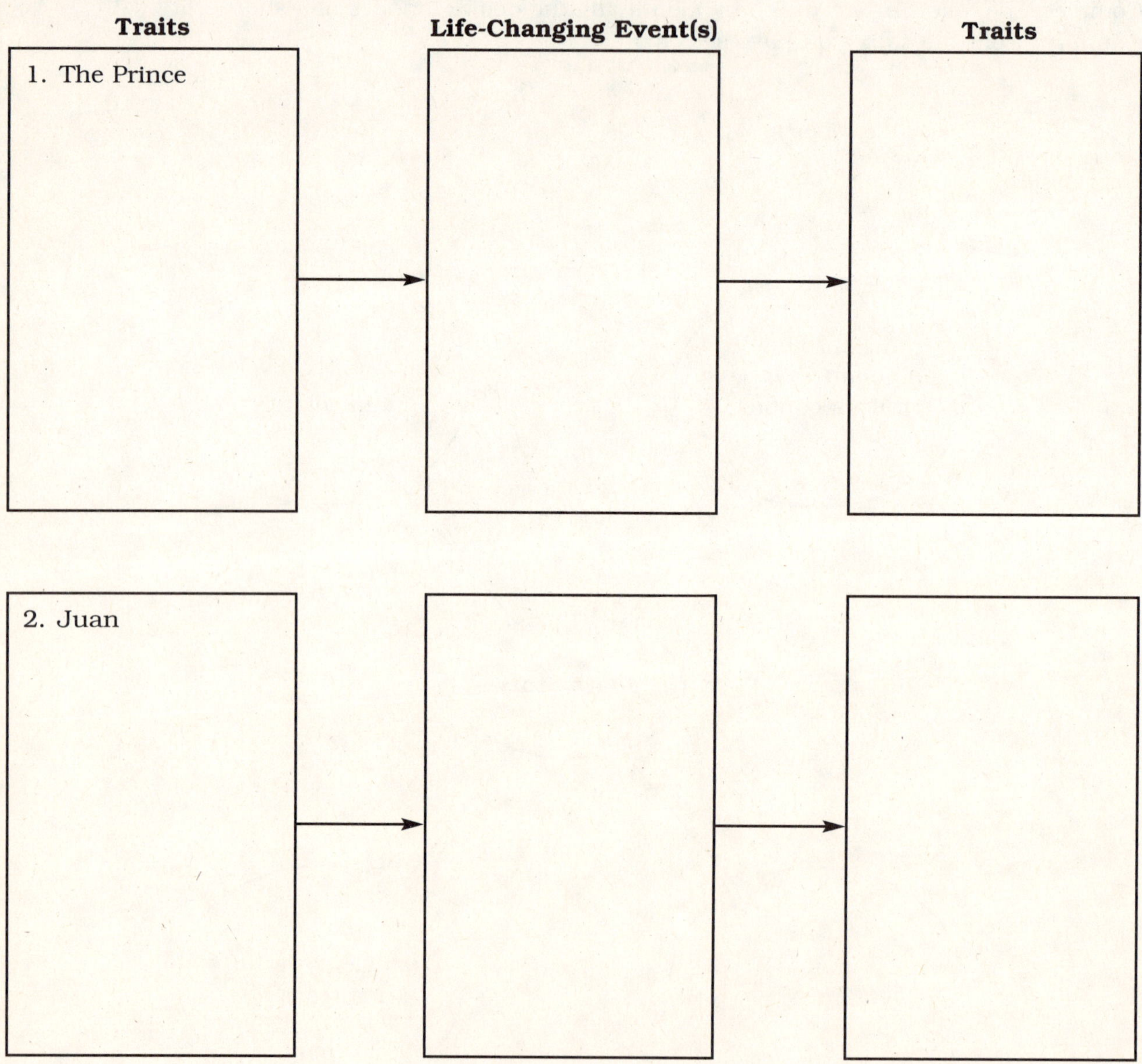

"The Marginal World" by Rachel Carson

Literary Analysis: Sensory Details in an Expository Essay

The main purpose of an expository essay is to inform or explain, but this doesn't mean the writer of an expository essay is not interested in engaging his or her readers with vivid language. **Sensory details,** for example, are words and phrases that appeal to your five senses—sight, touch, smell, hearing, and taste. These details make a work come alive to readers. You feel as if you are part of the scene when you can almost see, hear, feel, and smell what the writer describes.

DIRECTIONS: Find words and phrases in "The Marginal World" that appeal to your senses of sight, touch, and sound and record them in the following web. (The entire essay is filled with visual images. Choose two that you find especially vivid.)

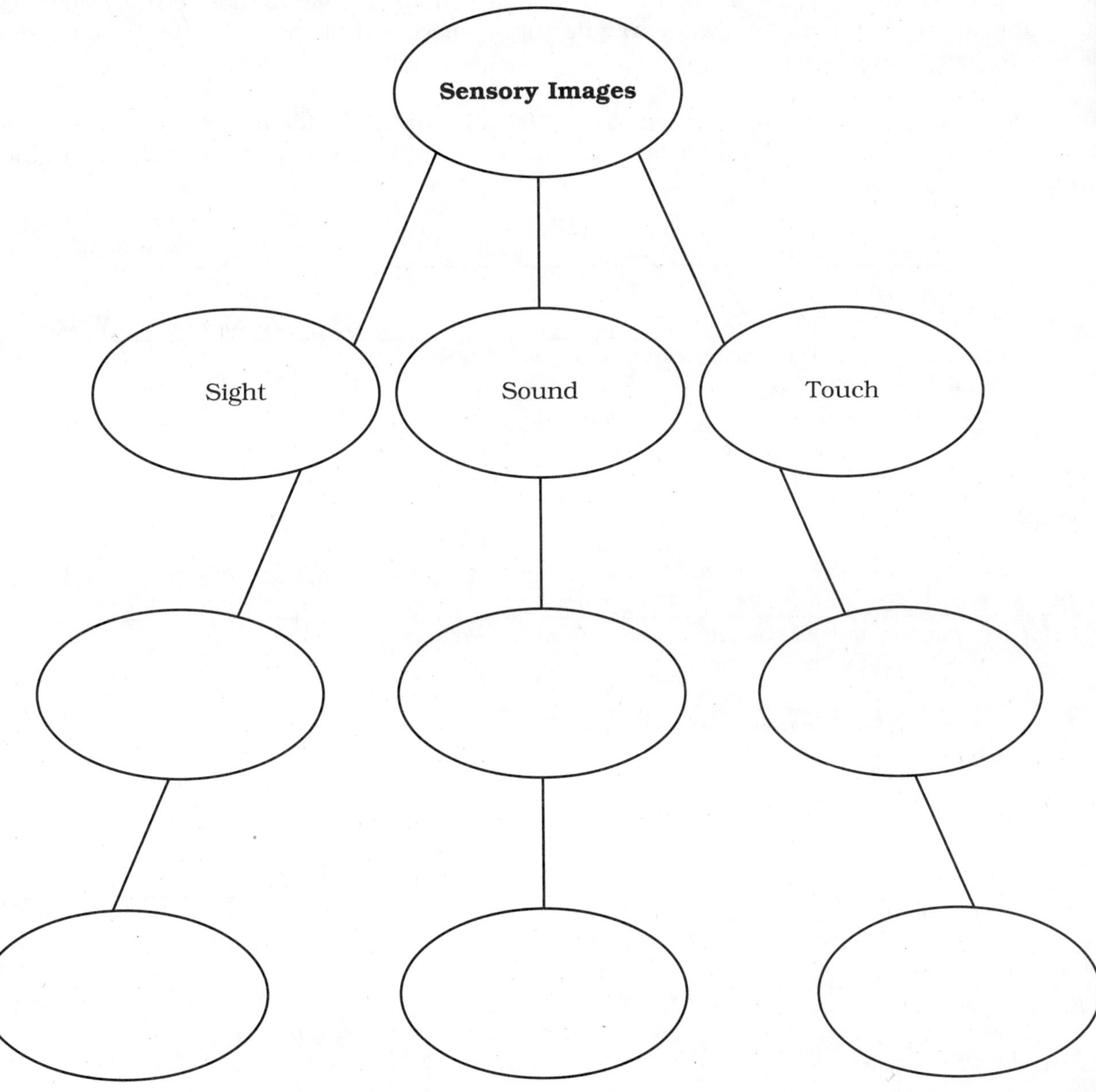

from *The Way to Rainy Mountain* by N. Scott Momaday
from "Nobel Lecture" by Alexander Solzhenitsyn
from "Keep Memory Alive" by Elie Wiesel

Literary Focus: The Persuasive Essay's Audience

The goal of a persuasive essay is to convince readers to do something or think about something in a particular way. Careful writers include examples, facts, and information that will help persuade readers. When writers includes these details, they often keep in mind the **audience**—the people who will be reading or listening to the work. A writer's audience may be mixed. Some members of the audience may be more knowledgeable than others.

Alexander Solzhenitsyn wants to persuade people of the power of the international writing community, some of whom are undoubtedly the audience for his essay. He says, "Today, between writers of one country and the readers and writers of another, there is an almost instantaneous reciprocity as I myself know." In the rest of this paragraph, Solzhenitsyn wants to convince his audience that he owes his fame and perhaps his life to those other writers who were able to respond in an immediate way during the period of his persecution at the hands of the Soviets.

DIRECTIONS: Read the following passages from "Nobel Lecture." Decide if each is directed more to a general audience or to the international community of writers. Place a checkmark in the appropriate column.

Directed At

Passage	General Audience	Writers
1. My books . . . have quickly found a responsive world readership.	✓	
2. Critical analysis of them has been undertaken by such leading Western writers as Heinrich Böll.		
3. During all these recent years, . . . I learned, to my complete surprise, of the support of the world's writing fraternity.		
4. On my fiftieth birthday I was astounded to receive greetings from well-known European writers.		
5. Mankind's salvation lies exclusively in everyone's making everything his business.		
6. Literature has the power . . . to help mankind see itself accurately.		
7. One word of truth outweighs the world.		
8. My being nominated for a Nobel Prize was originated not in the land where I live and write but by François Mauriac and his colleagues.		

"A Child's Christmas in Wales" by Dylan Thomas
"Marian Anderson: Famous Concert Singer" by Langston Hughes

Literary Focus: Diction in Autobiography

An autobiography is a personal account of the writer's own life, and the writer usually can take liberties that would probably not be considered acceptable for a biography. Dylan Thomas takes several liberties in his autobiography. For example, he seems to shun conventional language in favor of a more idiosyncratic one.

Diction is the writer's word choice. When you examine a writer's diction, you pay careful attention to the vocabulary used, the appropriateness of word choice, and the effects of the language.

DIRECTIONS: In the following chart, examine Thomas's diction. For each passage, write the possible meanings of Thomas's idiosyncratic language.

Unit 7: Nonfiction

Passage	Possible Meaning
1. All the Christmases roll down toward the two-tongued sea . . .	deceitful, as in "forked-tongued"; or a sea of many languages that "speaks" of danger as well as a place of recreation
2. They stop at the rim of the ice-edged, fish-freezing waves . . .	
3. In goes my hand into that wool-white bell-tongued ball of holidays . . .	
4. Years and years and years ago, . . . when we sang and wallowed all night and day in caves that smelt like Sunday afternoons in damp front farmhouse parlors . . .	
5. Snow grew overnight on the roofs of the houses like a pure and grandfather moss . . .	
6. Minutely white-ivied the walls and settled on the postman . . .	

                              Literary Analysis for Enrichment   **43**

"Flood" by Annie Dillard

Literary Analysis: Foreshadowing

Although Annie Dillard is writing a true description of the flooding of her familiar creek, she also employs literary techniques, especially foreshadowing. **Foreshadowing** involves the use of clues to suggest events that have yet to happen. This technique helps to introduce suspense and to keep the reader wondering what will happen next.

DIRECTIONS: Complete the following web by identifying clues from the beginning of the story that foreshadow Dillard's memory of the flood.

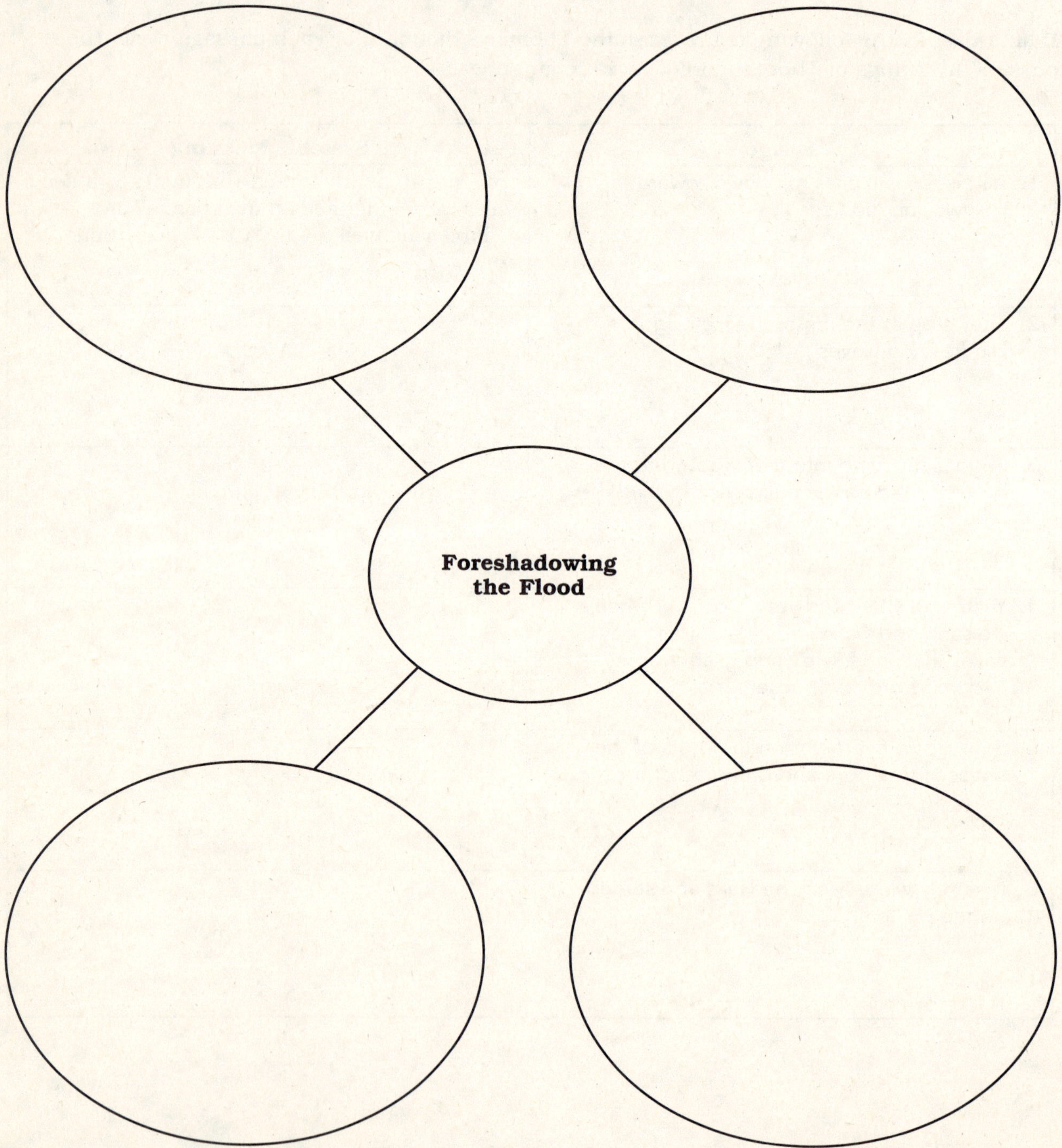

© Prentice-Hall, Inc.

"Star Wars—A Trip to a Far Galaxy That's Fun and Funny . . ." by Vincent Canby
***"Star Wars:* Breakthrough Film Still Has the Force"** by Roger Ebert

Literary Analysis: Comparing Persuasion

Critical reviews are common examples of persuasive writing. Persuasive writing has to answer the reader's question: "Why should I believe you?" The writer does this by providing reasons, the "because" the reader is looking for. When you read a piece of persuasive writing, you always should look for evidence that backs up the writer's statements.

DIRECTIONS: Compare these two pieces of persuasive writing by completing the following diagrams. For each work, identify the writer's main point (what he is trying to persuade you to believe) and then identify three pieces of evidence the writer uses to support his main point. When you are done, answer the question that follows.

"Marian Anderson: Famous Concert Singer"

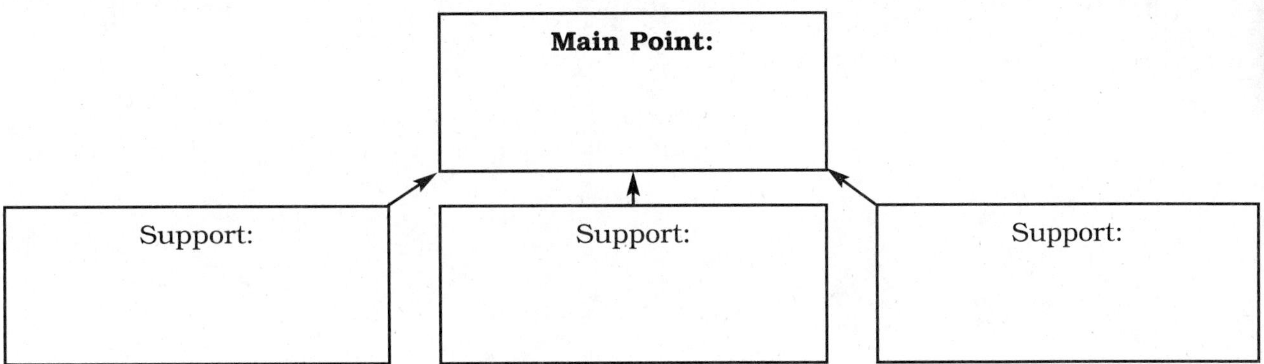

"Star Wars: Breakthrough Film Still Has the Force"

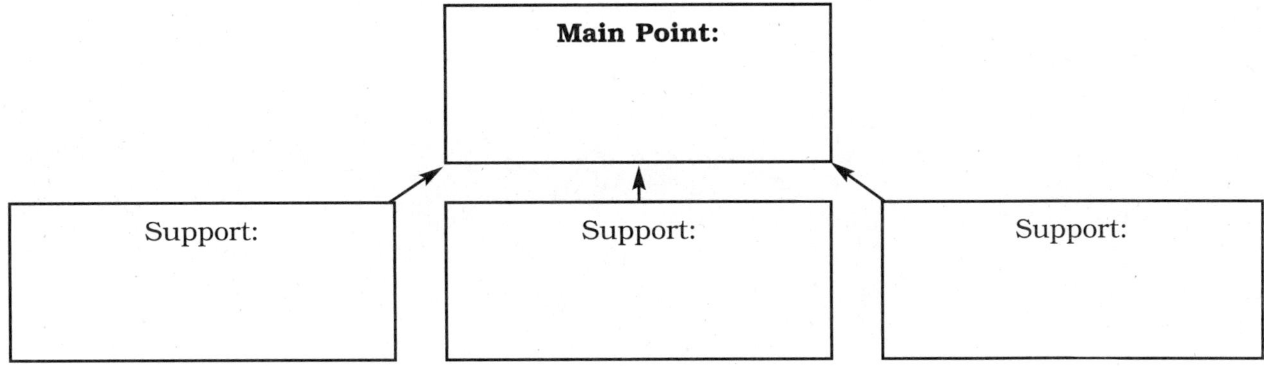

Although Langston Hughes's work is a biographical account of Marian Anderson career and Roger Ebert's work is a film review, they both try to persuade you to believe something. Which piece do find more persuasive. Why?

____

____

____

                    Literary Analysis for Enrichment **45**

"Mothers & Daughters" by Tillie Olsen and Estelle Jussim

Literary Analysis: Comparing Types of Essays

At first glance, a visual essay may seem to be very different from the other kinds of essays you've read. However, if you look carefully at the ways each kind of essay is structured, at the purposes each essay can serve, and the ways writers communicate meaning, you may notice more similarities than you expect.

DIRECTIONS: Use the following Venn diagram to compare a written essay with a visual essay. Record the differences in the outer portion of each circle. Record the similarities in the overlapping center space.

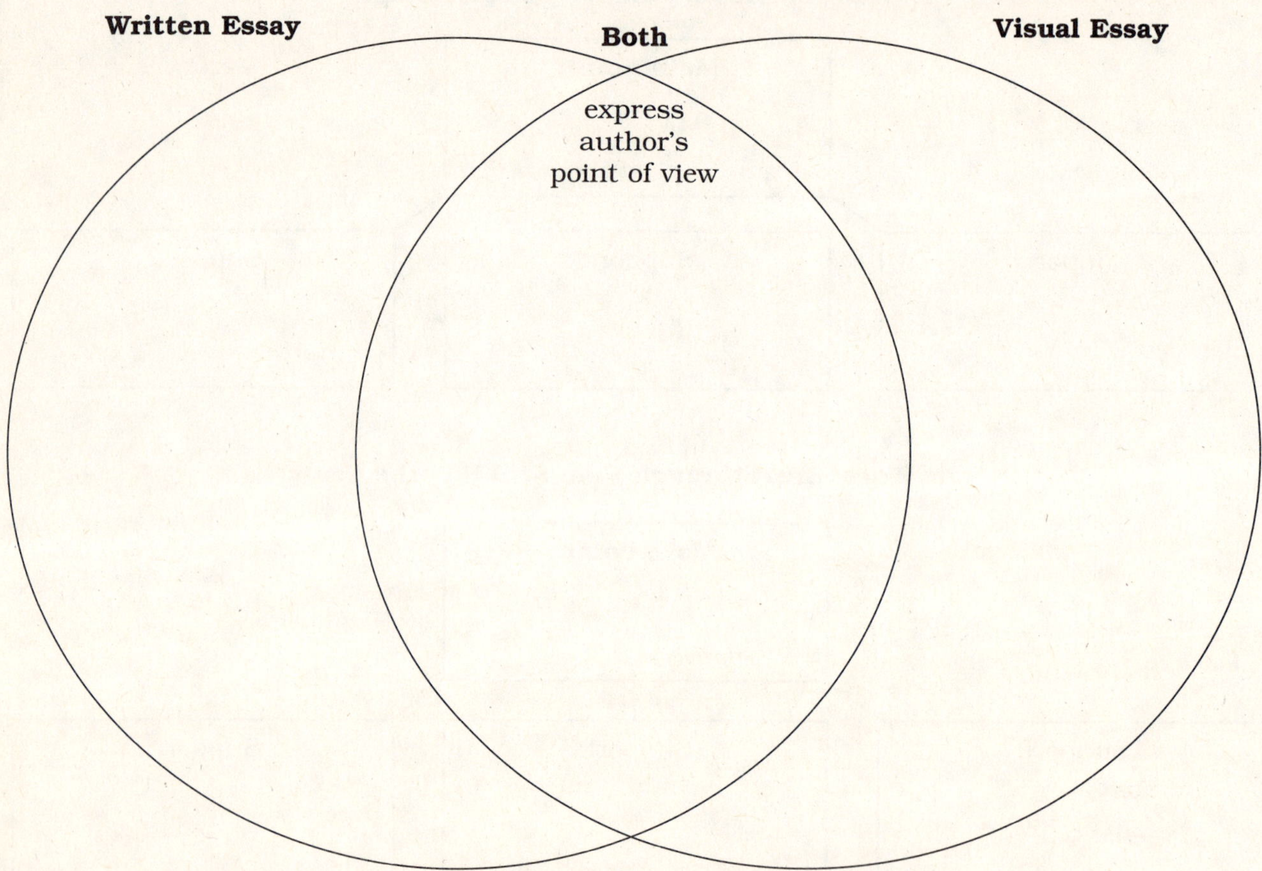

    © Prentice-Hall, Inc.

"Imitating Nature's Mineral Artistry" by Paul O'Neil
"Work That Counts" by Ernesto Ruelas Inzunza

Literary Analysis: Word Origins

A technical article is writing that explains procedures, gives instructions, or provides specialized information on a topic. You would expect to find a great deal of technical terms in these kind of articles. Technical words often have their roots in Greek, Latin, and other languages. For example, the word *opal* is derived from the Greek word *opallios*, meaning "stone" or "jewel."

DIRECTIONS: Use a dictionary to find the origin of the gem names below.

1. opal	from the Greek *opallios*, meaning "stone" or "jewel"
2. spinel	
3. diamond	
4. ruby	
5. silica	
6. titanium	

Antigone, **Prologue through Scene 2,** by Sophocles

Literary Analysis: Characterization

In the Greek tragedy *Antigone,* the protagonist is Antigone. She is the character you sympathize with and cheer for. The antagonist is the king, Creon. He's unforgivably prideful and his only goal in life is to preserve himself at all costs. Why do readers feel so strongly about these characters? It's because of their **characterization.** Sophocles develops the characters so their words and actions reach out and grab your thoughts and feelings and your heart and soul.

Writers can use two different kinds of characterization—direct and indirect. In **direct characterization,** the author comes right out and tells you what a character is like. In **indirect characterization,** a writer tells you how a character looks, what the character does and says, and how other characters react to him or her. You, the reader, must draw your own conclusions based on this indirect information. In *Antigone,* Sophocles relies primarily on indirect characterization.

DIRECTIONS: Complete the character webs for Antigone and Creon by first identifying character traits and then providing examples from the text to support each trait. The first one for each character has been done for you.

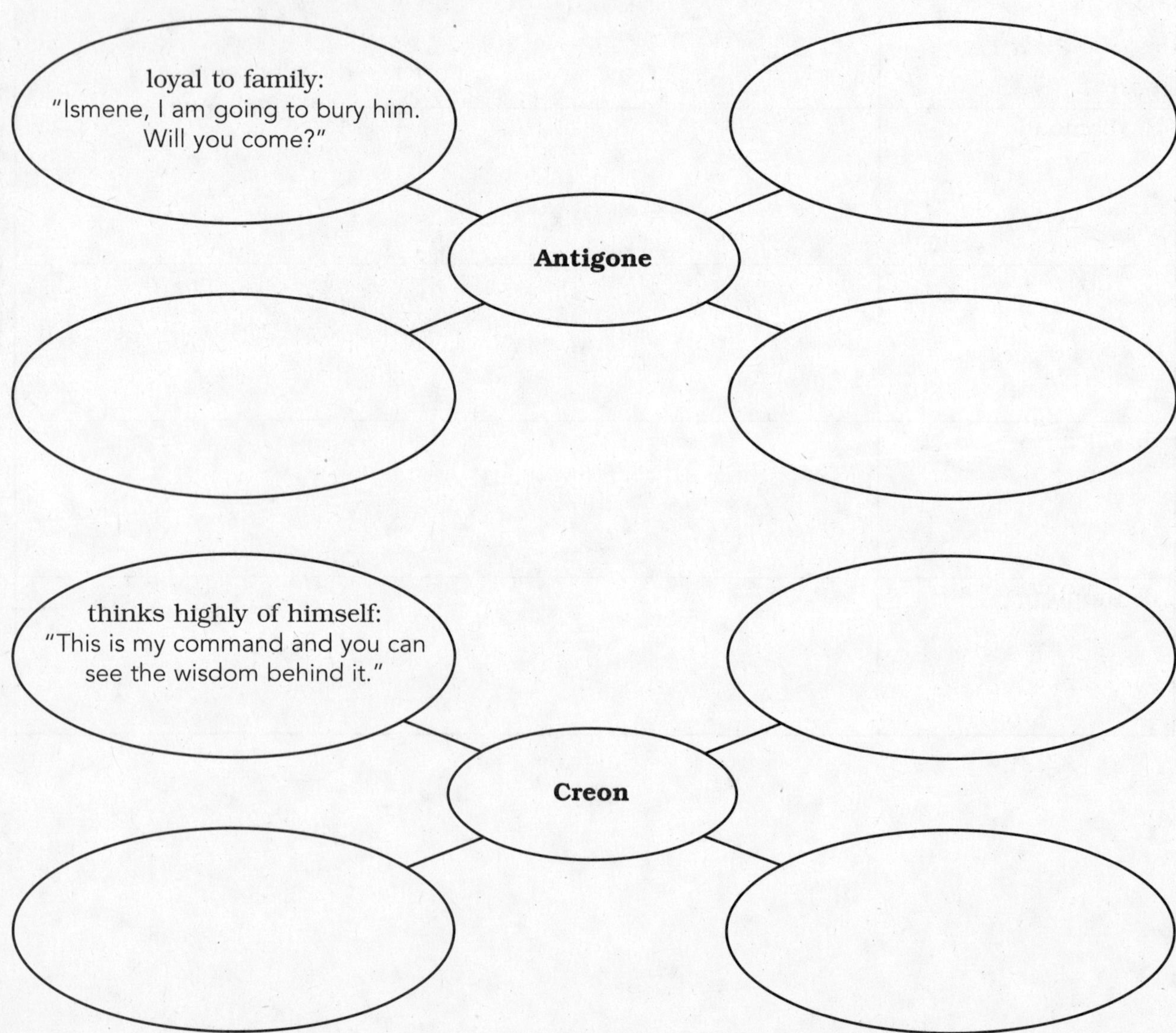

Antigone, **Scenes 3 through 5,** by Sophocles

Literary Analysis: Plot as an Element of Tragedy

The play *Antigone* is classified as a tragedy. The Greek philosopher Aristotle defined tragedy as "the imitation of an action that is serious, complete, and has sufficient size, in a language that is made sweet . . . exciting pity and fear, bringing about the catharsis of such emotions."

Aristotle also decreed that tragedies must always contain six elements: plot, character, thought, diction, music, and spectacle. In the tragedy *Antigone,* the plot is divided into five parts:

1. **Exposition**—provides background information; sets the scene for the conflict

2. **Rising Action**—begins when the conflict is introduced

3. **Climax**—occurs when the conflict is most intense

4. **Falling Action**—follows the climax and moves toward the end of the story

5. **Resolution**—shows how the story turned out

As you read the last three scenes of *Antigone,* notice the five stages of the plot and think about how they contribute to the intense "up and down" flow of a tragedy.

DIRECTIONS: First, review what takes place in the prologue and all five scenes of *Antigone.* Then complete the following diagram to show the events that helped build each stage in the plot of this tragedy. You may need to list more than one event in several of the categories.

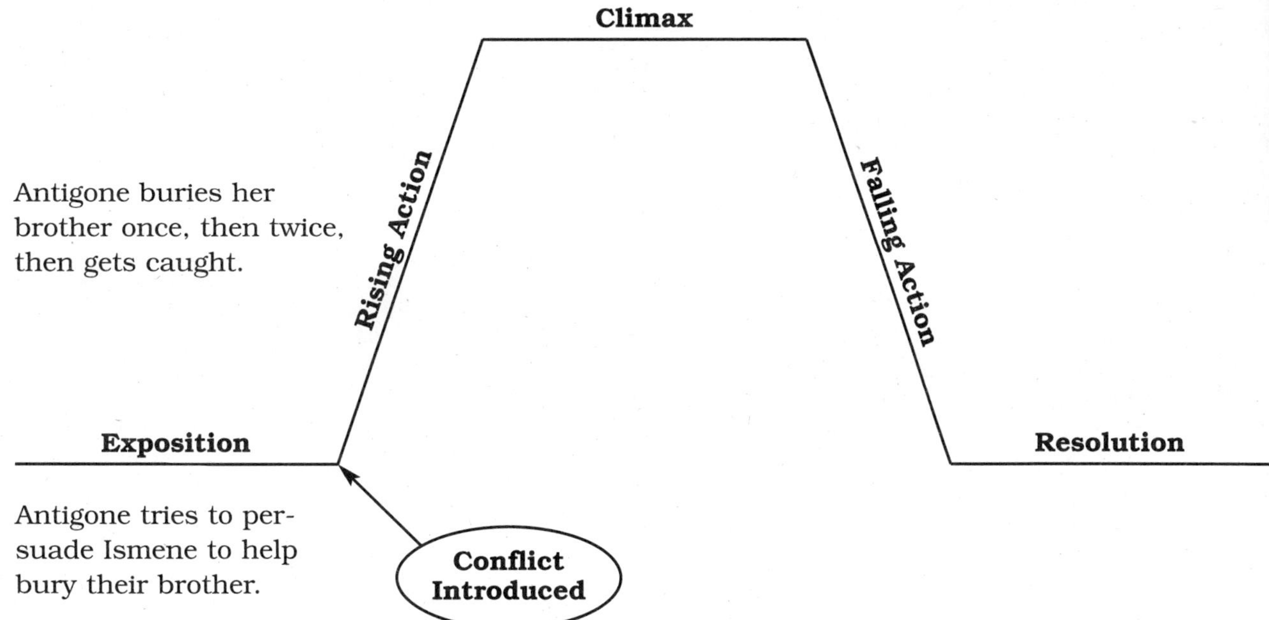

Unit 8: Drama

The Tragedy of Julius Caesar, Act I, by William Shakespeare

Literary Analysis: Wordplay

Shakespeare's opening scenes in Julius Caesar serve as his exposition. The **exposition,** or opening part of the play, introduces the characters, the setting, and the situation. When you read these scenes, they may seem very lighthearted to you. Watch the language closely for Shakespeare's clever use of irony, puns, and **plays on words.** Shakespeare uses these techniques to tease his readers and keep them on the lookout for hidden or double meanings. As you read through Act I, use the stage directions and text aids to see if you can catch Shakespeare's wordplay.

DIRECTIONS: After you read Act I, complete in the following chart by explaining the first two examples of Shakespeare's wordplay. Then complete the chart by choosing three of your own examples from the play.

Wordplay	Explanation
1. cobbler	Shakespeare uses this word's double meanings (mender of shoes or clumsy worker) to build a lighthearted dialogue.
2. mettle	
3.	
4.	
5.	

The Tragedy of Julius Caesar, Act II, by William Shakespeare

Literary Analysis: Identifying Meter and Feet in Poetry

For the most part, Shakespeare wrote *Julius Caesar* in unrhymed **iambic pentameter.**
Iambic means that an unaccented syllable is followed by an accented syllable: "By all / the gods." A *foot* is one set of these unaccented and accented syllables: "By all" or "the gods."
Pentameter means "a rhythmical pattern using five feet": "By all / the gods / the Ro / mans bow / before. . . ."
Here's a list of other categories of feet and meter.

<table>
<tr><td>Feet—rhythmic units</td><td colspan="2">Meter—the type and number of
rhythmic units in a line</td></tr>
<tr><td rowspan="2">Iambic—unstressed, stressed: away</td><td colspan="2">Monometer: verse written in one-foot lines:
All things
Must pass
Away</td></tr>
<tr><td colspan="2">Dimeter: verse written in two-foot lines:
Paula / Thompson
What do / you know</td></tr>
<tr><td>Trochaic—stressed, unstressed: wonder</td><td colspan="2">Trimeter: verse written in three-foot lines:
I know / not whom / I meet
I know / not where / I go</td></tr>
<tr><td rowspan="2">Anapestic—unstressed, unstressed,
stressed: contradict</td><td colspan="2">Tetrameter: verse written in four-foot lines</td></tr>
<tr><td colspan="2">Pentameter: verse written in five-foot lines</td></tr>
<tr><td rowspan="3">Dactyllic—stressed, unstressed,
unstressed: merrily</td><td colspan="2">Hexameter: verse written in six-foot lines</td></tr>
<tr><td colspan="2">Heptameter: verse written in seven-foot lines</td></tr>
<tr><td colspan="2">Free verse: poetry that does not have a regular
meter</td></tr>
</table>

DIRECTIONS: Review the poems in Units 3 and 4, keeping the principles of feet and meter in mind. Then list lines of poetry you find that fit the following descriptions.

Type of Meter	Example
1. Trochaic tetrameter	
2. Iambic tetrameter	
3. Free verse	

***The Tragedy of Julius Caesar*, Act III,** by William Shakespeare

Literary Analysis: Comparing Dramatic Speeches

All three special types of speeches—the aside, the soliloquy, and the monologue—can be found in Shakespearean drama.

DIRECTIONS: Compare the three kinds of speeches by completing the following Venn diagram. In the overlapping section on the circles, identify the similarities among all three kinds of speeches. In the outer portion of each circle, identify the differences.

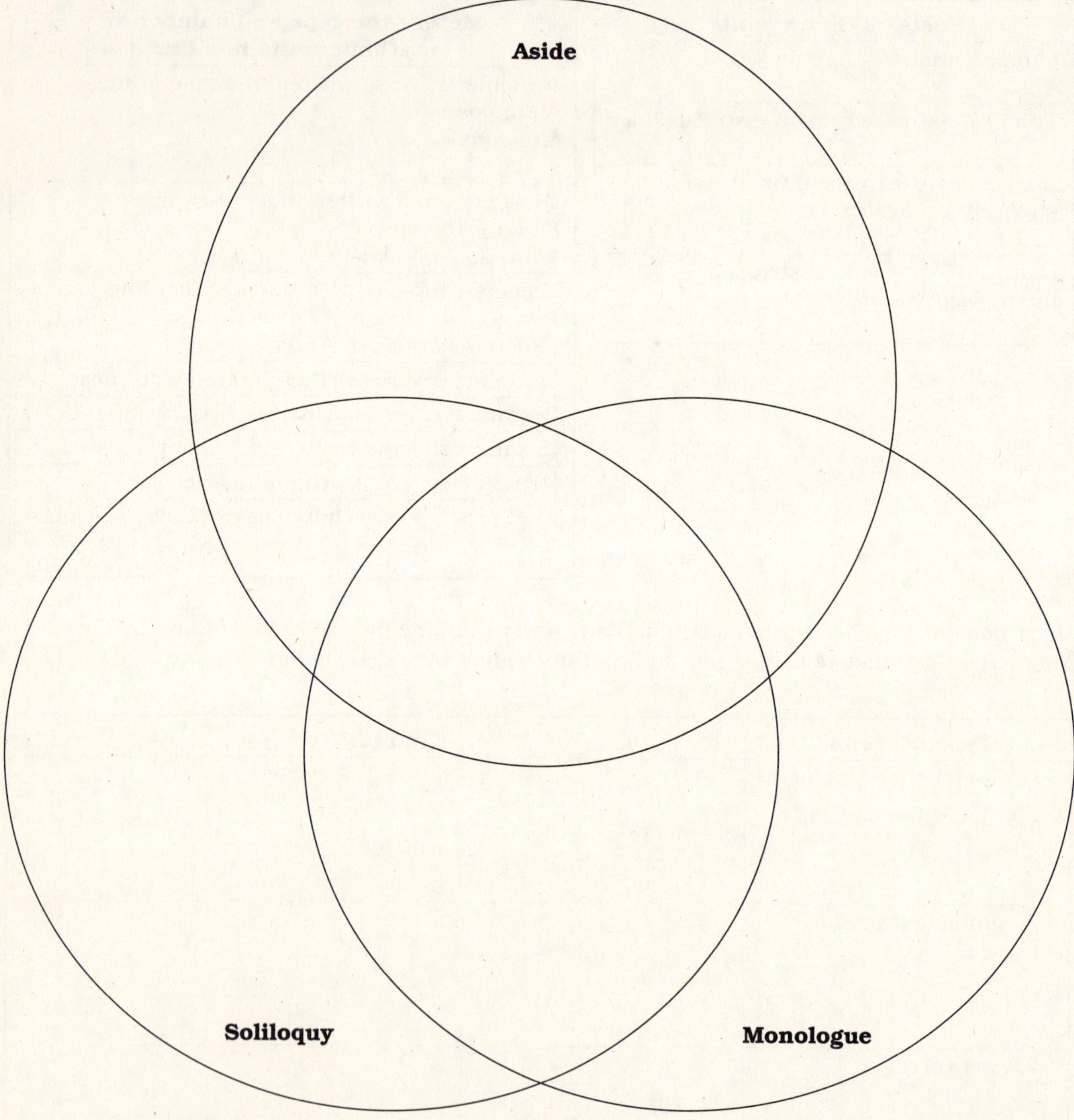

The Tragedy of Julius Caesar, **Act IV,** by William Shakespeare

Literary Analysis: Conflict and Dramatic Foils

Conflict is what drives the action of all stories, novels, and plays. Conflict can arise from a variety of causes. One typical way a writer will create conflict is through the characters in his or her work. When characters in a play have contrasting character traits and personalities, they are known as **dramatic foils.** By using a foil, a writer can call the reader's attention to a main character's particular qualities and traits, as well as set up dramatic conflict.

DIRECTIONS: Brutus and Antony are dramatic foils in *The Tragedy of Julius Caesar.* Compare and contrast these two characters in the following chart. You can refer to Act I through Act IV to complete the diagram. Then use the likenesses and differences to draw conclusions about both characters.

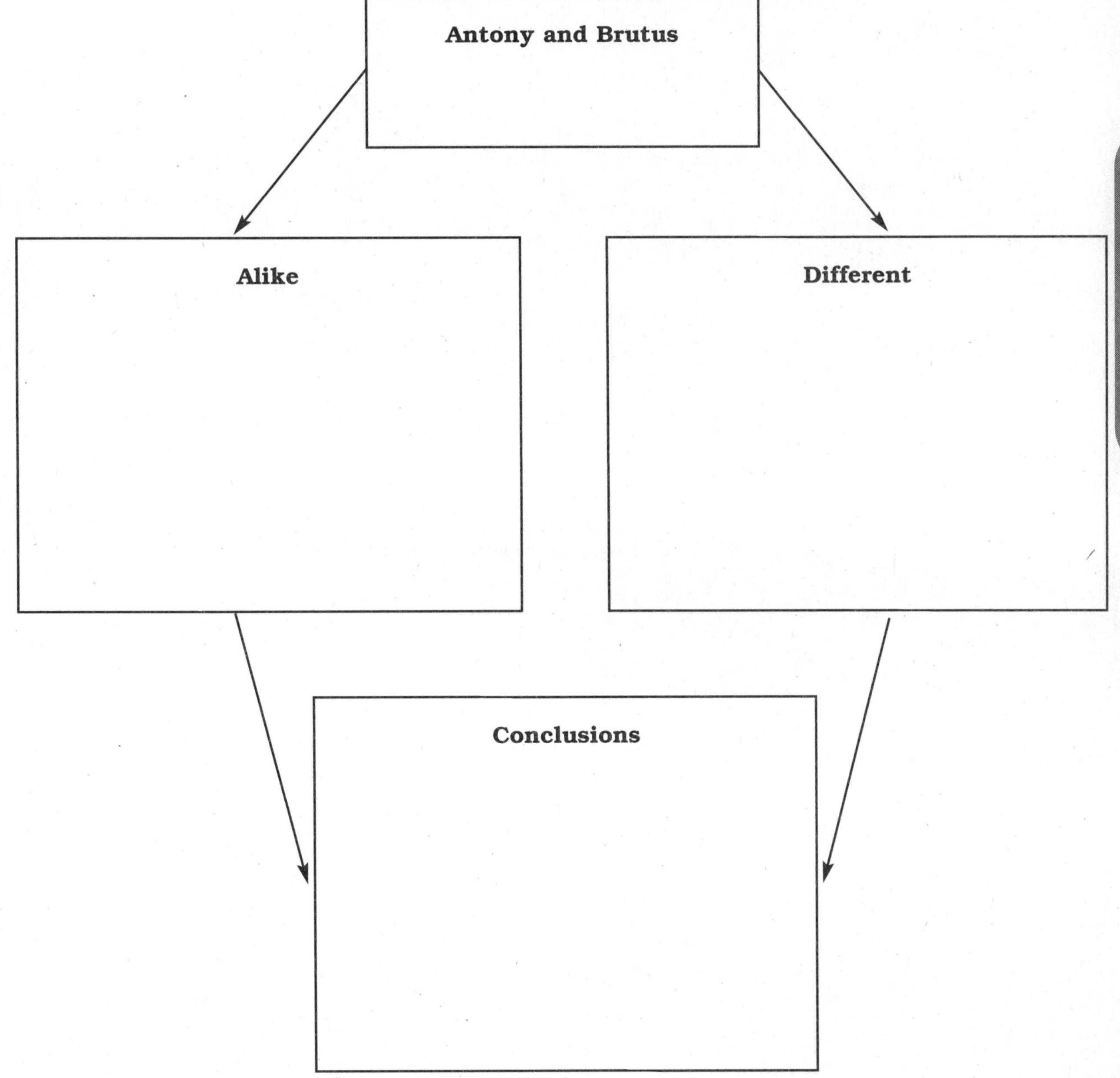

   Literary Analysis for Enrichment   **53**

The Tragedy of Julius Caesar, Act V, by William Shakespeare

Literary Analysis: Round Characters in Tragedies

In tragedies, such as *Julius Caesar,* main characters become involved in struggles that always end in disaster. Often, these characters have tragic flaws, or weaknesses, that lead to their downfall. Writers create "round" characters for these tragic roles. A **round character** has both faults and virtues—bad points as well as good points. It's usually easy to identify with round characters, because we tend to be round, too—people with both good traits and not-so-good traits.

Brutus is a good example of a round character in a tragic role. Shakespeare shows Brutus's strengths and his weaknesses. We can relate to a guy who gets drawn into the wrong crowd when he's really trying to do the right thing. We feel badly when we see unavoidable disaster ahead for someone who means well but has made some serious mistakes.

DIRECTIONS: Complete the following character web for the tragic character Brutus.

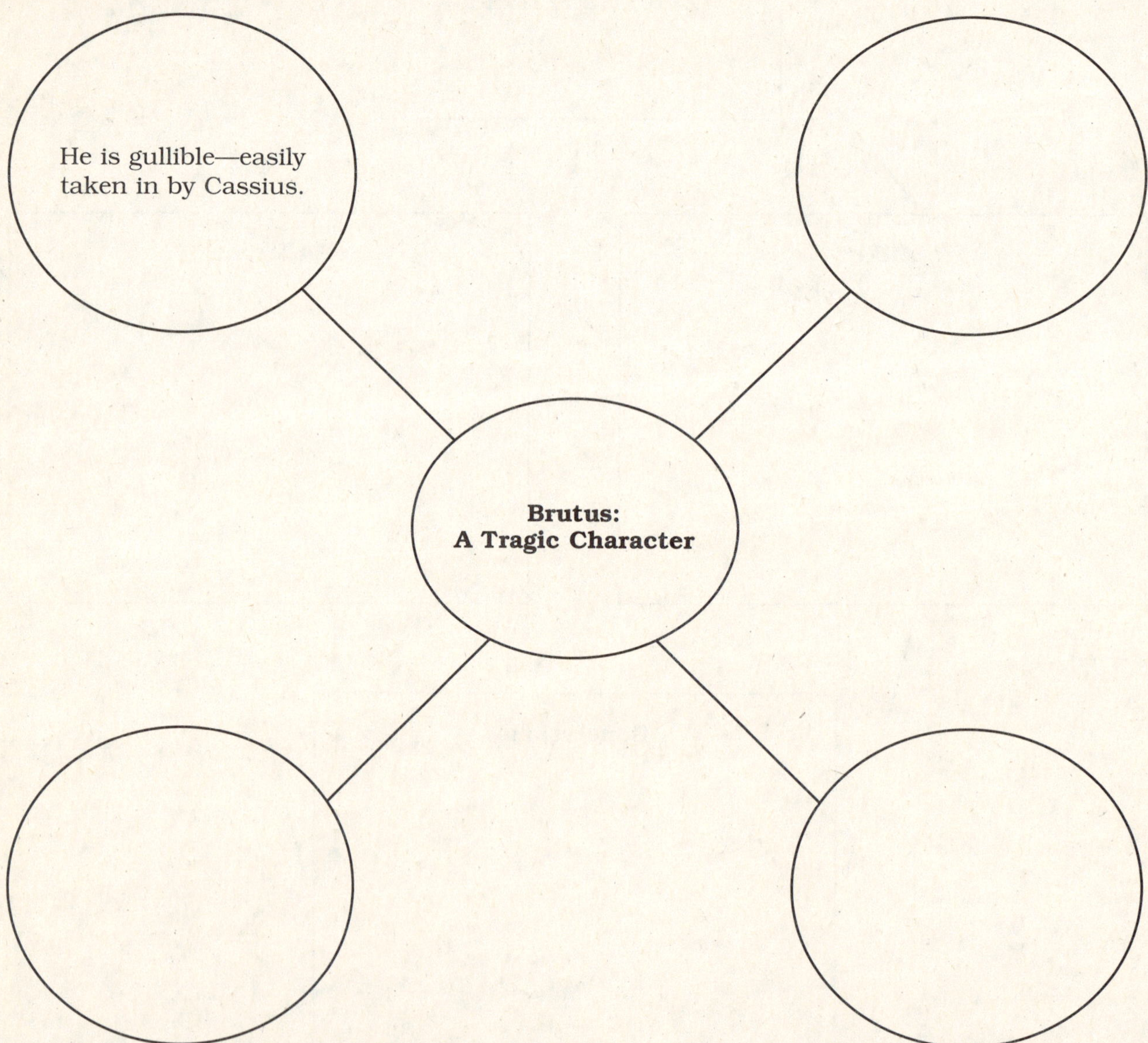

"The Stolen Child" by William Butler Yeats

Literary Analysis: Refrain

The atmosphere or mood of a poem can be created in a number of ways. In addition to sensory language and sound devices, a poet can establish an atmosphere by repeating specific lines in the poem. A **refrain** is a phrase or verse in a poem that recurs at the end of a stanza. A poet often uses a refrain to reinforce a particular idea or image in the poem.

DIRECTIONS: Identify the refrain in "The Stolen Child" by writing it in the following box. Then answer the questions that follow.

1. Why do you think the refrain is set in italics? ___________________________________
____
____
____

2. What is the meaning of the refrain? Paraphrase it in your own words. ______________
____
____
____

3. Why do you think Yeats chose to repeat these lines? _____________________________
____
____
____

4. Why does the refrain change the last time it appears in the poem? _________________
____
____
____

"In Flanders Fields" by John McCrae
"The Kraken" by Alfred, Lord Tennyson
"Reapers" by Jean Toomer
"Meeting at Night" by Robert Browning
"Prayer of First Dancers" Traditional Navajo Chant

Literary Analysis: Comparing Alliteration, Consonance, and Assonance

Poets often use devices in their poems that call attention to the sounds and musical qualities of letters, words, and phrases. **Alliteration, consonance,** and **assonance** are three devices that involve the repetition of letter sounds. Poets typically use these devices to emphasize particular words that have important emotional or thematic meaning in a poem.

DIRECTIONS: Complete the following chart by identifying examples of alliteration, consonance, and assonance in "Reapers" and "Meeting at Night." Then answer the question that follows.

Poem	Alliteration	Consonance	Assonance
1. "Reapers"	sound of steel on stones		
2. "Meeting at Night"			

3. Read both poems aloud. What are the effects of these musical devices?

____

____

____

____

"The Wind—tapped like a tired Man" by Emily Dickinson
"A Pace Like That" by Yehuda Amichai
"Metaphor" by Eve Merriam
"Right Hand" by Philip Fried

Literary Analysis: Figurative Language and Theme

Looking at the figurative language in a poem can help you determine the poem's theme. The **theme** of a poem is the central message about life that is communicated by the poet. The theme is not simply a summary or a paraphrase, but a generalization about human existence. Sometimes, a poem's theme is stated directly. Other times, the theme is implied. Think about what the poet is trying to say to you and what lessons you can learn from the poem.

DIRECTIONS: For each of the poems listed in the following chart, identify two examples of figurative language. Name the type of figurative language each example represents and then state the theme of the poem. When you have finished, answer the question that follows.

Poem	Example of Figurative Language	Type of Figurative Language	Theme
1. "The Wind—tapped like a tired Man"	a. The Wind—tapped like a tired Man b.	a. personification and simile b.	
2. "A Pace Like That"	a. b.	a. b.	
3. "Metaphor"	a. b.	a. b.	
4. "Right Hand"	a. b.	a. b.	

5. How does a poet's use of figurative language contribute to the theme of a poem?

____

____

____

"La Belle Dame sans Merci" by John Keats
"Danny Deever" by Rudyard Kipling

Literary Analysis: Comparing Narrative and Dramatic Poetry

A **narrative** poem, as its name indicates, tells a story. These poems typically have the same features as other pieces of narrative writing—a plot, setting, and characters. A **dramatic** poem may or may not have a plot, but it does have characters who speak. The dialogue of these characters conveys the events in the poem.

DIRECTIONS: Compare the elements of narrative and dramatic poetry by completing the Venn diagram. Then answer the question that follows.

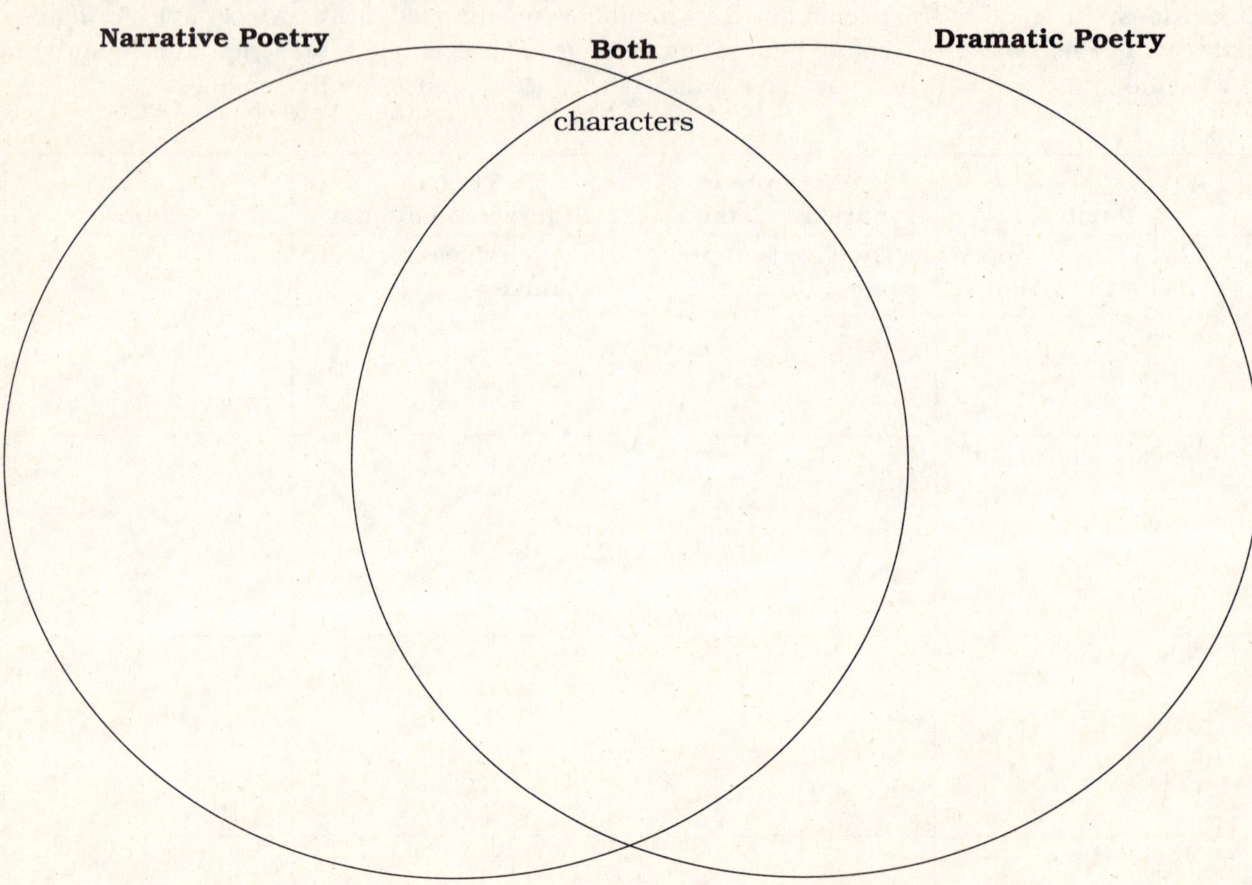

Do you think a dramatic poem could also be considered a narrative poem? Explain?

____

____

____

"The Guitar" by Federico García Lorca
"Making a Fist" by Naomi Shihab Nye
"Jade Flower Palace" by Tu Fu
"The Moon at the Fortified Pass" by Li Po
"What Are Friends For" by Rosellen Brown
"Some Like Poetry" by Wisława Szymborska

Literary Analysis: Imagery in Lyric Poetry

Lyric poetry was originally meant to be sung to musical accompaniment. It is a type of poetry rich in musical devices, or techniques that call attention to the sounds musical qualities of letters, words, and phrases. However, lyric poetry can appeal to all of your five sense, not just sound. Lyric poetry explores a particular experience and uses vivid imagery to make reading the poem a powerful sensory experience.

DIRECTIONS: Complete the following chart by examining the imagery in one of the poems in this section. Choose a poem and identify the sensory details by writing them in the appropriate column of the chart.

Poem: ____

Sight	Sound	Touch	Taste	Smell

Unit 9: Poetry

Sonnet 18 by William Shakespeare
"The Waking" by Theodore Roethke
Tanka by Ki no Tsurayuki and Priest Jakuren
Haiku by Matsuo Bashō and Kobayshi Issa

Literary Analysis: Poetry

Poetry represents one of the three major kinds of literature. The elements of poetry include:

- **Form**—written in **lines,** which are divided into **stanzas**

- **Sound devices**—create specific sounds effects through techniques such as **rhyme, rhythm,** and **repetition**

- **Imagery**—creates a picture in the reader's mind through details that appeal to the five senses

- **Figurative language**—comparisons between unlike things, including **simile, metaphor,** and **personification**

DIRECTIONS: Complete the following diagram by identifying the poetic elements in two poems of your choice. Write your answers at the end of each spoke. You'll have to copy the chart for the second poem.) One of the poems should be from this section; the other can be from this unit.

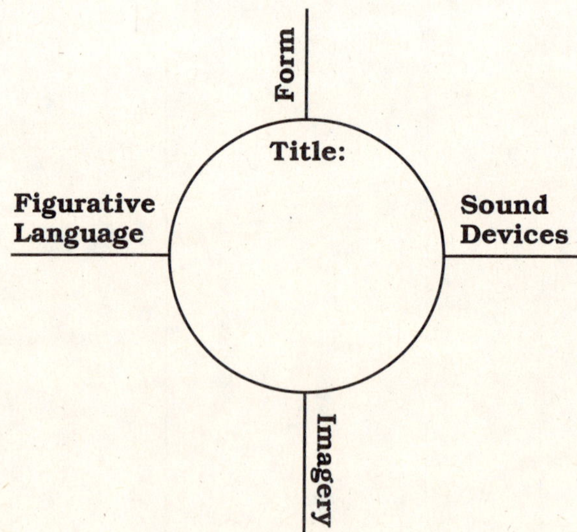

from *Don Quixote* by Miguel de Cervantes

Literary Analysis: Narrator

In a parody like *Don Quixote*, it is useful to identify the narrator—the speaker or the character who tells the story. The writer's choice of narrator determines the story's point of view, which in turn determines the type and amount of information the writer can reveal. For instance, the writer can use **first-person narration** to reveal the thoughts and feelings of just that one character in the story. However, the writer also can tell the story through an character outside the story, known as a **third-person narration,** to reveal what all the characters are thinking and feeling. This type of narration is useful for setting up dramatic irony, in which the reader knows more about the truth of a situation than a character does.

DIRECTIONS: In the following chart, answer each question about the narrator of *Don Quixote*. Make sure to support each of your answers. When you are finished, answer the question that follows.

Question	Answer	How You Know
1. What kind of narrator is used?	outside observer who can read characters' thoughts	As the narrator tells Don Quixote's story, we learn what Don Quixote's thinking.
2. What is the narrator's tone?		
3. What is the narrator's attitude toward Don Quixote?		
4. How is dramatic irony revealed by the narrator?		
5. What is the writer's viewpoint toward chivalry, as shown by the narrator?		

6. Do you think the story would be as humorous if it were told solely from Don Quixote's point of view? Why or why not?

____

____

____

   Literary Analysis for Enrichment   **61**

"Morte d'Arthur" by Alfred, Lord Tennyson
"Arthur Becomes King of Britain" from ***The Once and Future King***
by T. H. White

Literary Analysis: Comparing Elements of Fantasy

Legends, such as those involving King Arthur, often contain elements of **fantasy**—things that could not occur in real life. Recognizing the importance of fantasy elements in a legend can help you better understand its meaning.

DIRECTIONS: In the following chart, list fantasy elements from each work and the importance of each element to the plot. When you are finished, answer the question that follows.

	Fantasy Elements	**Importance to Plot**
"Morte d'Arthur"	1.	
	2.	
"Arthur Becomes King of Britain"	3.	
	4.	
	5.	

6. How do the fantasy elements surrounding the sword add to the legend of King Arthur?

____

____

"Rama's Initiation" from *the Ramayana* by R. K. Narayan

Literary Analysis: Comparing Characters

Characters in fiction can be described as round or flat. **Round characters** display a range of good and bad traits—they have faults as well as virtues. In contrast, **flat characters** exhibit only a few traits, which are either good or bad. Flat characters often operate as symbols or serve as comic relief because of their one-dimensionality.

DIRECTIONS: In the following chart, describe the characters from the works you have read. First, identify their main traits. Then decide if they are round or flat characters. Finally, support your answers. The first one has been done for you. When you are finished, answer the question that follows.

Character	Main Traits	Round or Flat	How You Know
Don Quixote 1. Don Quixote 2. Sancho	imaginative, impractical, romantic, foolish	round	His behavior becomes more extreme as the story progresses.
"Morte d'Arthur" 3. King Arthur 4. Sir Bedivere			
"Arthur Becomes King of Britain" 5. King Pellinore 6. the Wart			
"Rama's Initiation" 7. Rama 8. Thataka			

9. Why do you think storytellers include flat characters when telling long adventures and epics?

____

____

____

from *Sundiata: An Epic of Old Mali* retold by D. T. Niane

Literary Analysis: Setting and the Epic Conflict

The **setting** is the time and place of a story. The setting of an epic can provide important clues about the storyteller's purpose and the culture in which the epic was told. Paying attention to the setting can help you predict the types of obstacles an epic hero might face and how he or she might overcome them.

DIRECTIONS: In the following chart, describe how each setting affects the plot of *Sundiata*. The first one has been done for you. When you are finished, answer the question that follows.

Setting	How the Setting Affects the Plot
Beginning 1. Sogolon Kedjou's house, when Djata is three	Djata is mocked whenever Sassouma goes by his mother's house, because he can't walk.
Middle 2. anteroom of a blacksmith's house, a year or two later 3. king's palace, when Djata is around seven 4. backyard of the palace, same year 5. Sogolon Kedjou's little garden behind the village, same year 6. Sogolon Kedjou's hut, same day as #5 7. royal forges, same day as #5	
Climax 8. mother's hut, same day as #5	
Resolution 9. young baobab tree, same day as #5	

10. Why is it important for readers to picture the setting in their minds?

____

____

